D0463886

ENDORSEMENTS

"Jim's deep understanding of friendship is the connection God intended, His road map of how life is intended."

John Knox Jr, President and CEO, Sure Tech

"*Covenant Friendship* is an eye-opener, or I should say, a SELF-OPENER that deserves our time and thought. It is an important invitation to venture forth slowly but purposefully to realize trust in yourself and others. Our Bible is strongly relational, and Jim has the talent to meaningfully illuminate examples of relational Bible verses that I had previously not digested."

Yvonne Streit, Brookwood Community

"Jim Jackson is a preacher whose deep wisdom is rooted in a life steeped in the study of Scripture and his own commitment to follow Jesus. *Covenant Friendship* grows out of his personal desire to overcome loneliness and form authentic friendships. It will inspire, encourage, teach, and offer hope to those who seek deep friendships themselves. This is a book for both individual reflection and study and for small groups and Sunday School classes."

Bishop Janice R. Huie, Texas Annual Conference, United Methodist Church

"Dr. Jim Jackson has served for over a decade as both pastor and valued friend to my family and me. Through this book on the sustaining strength of covenant friendship, Jim captures much of what we learned from him and generously shares his wisdom with us all."

Larry Kellner, Chair of the Board, Sabre Holdings Company
and former Chairman and CEO, Continental Airlines

"Jim's profound clarity of thought illuminates every page. His words will capture your heart. With this title at your bedside, Jim is always there for you in times of trouble. His love for God shines throughout this supportive book—a brilliant companion that will help you navigate your life with amazing grace."

Bob Brockman, Chairman and CEO, Reynolds and Reynolds

"The quality of our lives is a direct function of the persons we choose to have in our lives. *Covenant Friendship* is the right book to help you choose the right persons to be in your life for the right reasons. Finally! Bless God!"

Kirbyjon H. Caldwell, Senior Pastor,
Windsor Village United Methodist Church, Houston, Texas

"Dr. Jim Jackson manages to blend deeply personal and powerful self-disclosure with substantive Biblical insights. With this 'teaching' memoir, he deftly expands his sermon series on covenant friendship to give us an important gift: the gift of making sure we truly value the nourishing, in fact, critical role that true covenant friends play in our emotional, mental, and spiritual health."

Sharon Birkman Fink, CEO, Birkman International

COVENANT FRIENDSHIP

An Ex-Loner's Guide to Authentic Friendships

Dr. James F. (Jim) Jackson

Banlican House Publishers
HOUSTON, TEXAS

COVENANT FRIENDSHIP

Banlican House Publishers, Houston, Texas

Library of Congress Control Number: 2014903209

ISBN: 978-0-9915638-0-7

Design: Limb Design

Printed in the United States of America
14 15 16 17 18 19 [Printer Code] 6 5 4 3 2 1

IN HONOR OF

Susan, my covenant wife;

Carolyn and Jimmy, Meg and Jared, our children;

Sadie, Charlie, Lainey, Oliver, and Savannah, our grandchildren;

and

our covenant friends

ACKNOWLEDGMENTS

I am indebted to many people for making this book possible. Special thanks are due to Leslie and Tom Hix, Linda and John Knox, and Beth and Schuyler Tilney for allowing Susan and me to use their homes so that I could hide away and write.

And I am also grateful to Carl Andersen, Sharon Fink, Susan Jackson, Bob Johnson, Bob Larkins, Linda Limb, Bob Lindsey, Barbara O'Quinn, Allen Quine, and Teresa Rossy for reading the book while it was in progress and making recommendations. I hope each of these people knows the special contribution they made and how grateful I am to them.

CONTENTS

INTRODUCTION

This book was born out of my personal struggle. It is my hope that other loners, either by disposition or habit, will find in the pages that follow the practical help needed to change their relational course.

I make no claim to superior insights on the subject of friendship. Throughout human history, sages have written at a depth that I am not capable of duplicating. I have read what classical thinkers had to say on the subject—Plato, Aristotle, Cicero, Ambrose, Augustine, Aquinas, Montaigne, Bacon, Emerson, and Thoreau—to name a few. Their insights gave me pause as to whether I had anything noteworthy to add to the conversation. Ultimately I decided to put my thoughts on paper for two reasons: first, to keep a vow to write out my ideas; and second, because I believe I have some unique biblical insights to offer to relational seekers.

The thesis of the book is that none of us has a greater need— outside of a redemptive union with Jesus (Colossians 1:15)—than covenant friends. God did not intend for us to live in isolation or uncultivated relationships. We all hunger to know and be known, to love and be loved, to be a friend and to have a friend. The divine plan for us includes committed companionship. God said, "It is not good for humans to be alone" (Genesis 2:18).

Psychologists agree that most of us develop false selves, or masks, at an early age. It is a survival mechanism. We do it to fit in with groups whose acceptance we crave. Sometimes our identities are assigned by family members. Other roles emerge as attempts to negotiate the crosscurrents of life. It is easy for us to assume these false selves are our true self. As we mature, the more emotionally healthy among us discover who we are, discard our masks, and live consistently with our true nature. This psychological breakthrough occurs through reflection and relational transparency. Ordinarily the catalyst for this self-integration is friendship.

Many times, however, people enter adulthood believing the roles they have created are their true self. These unfortunate adults must face some sort of crisis or failure for their false selves to be brought to awareness. One common crisis is marriage. The spouse discovers that the person they married is different from the person they dated. He or she begins to ask, "What happened to the person I fell in love with?" Sometimes the marriage is threatened because both spouses feel this way. They are essentially two false selves trying to live in intimacy.

I am more and more convinced that before we engage in covenant marriage, we must experience covenant friendship. Covenant friendship is the means by which we come to terms with the false selves we have adopted, discard them, and live authentically. This deep internal work cannot be done in isolation. When we attempt to do the work of transformation in secret, it is because we fear exposure and shame.

This book is designed to help you build covenant friendships through which you are safe to come out of hiding, tell your friends who you think you are, and have your friends interpret back to you the self you have experienced. Because of the conviction that covenant friendship needs to occur before covenant marriage, this book does not address marital friendship directly. However, the same relational principles apply, since the primary basis of marriage is friendship.

It is my hope that these pages will create in you a desire for relational intimacy and build a road map for establishing covenant friendships. I have a friend who is fond of saying, "You can lead a horse to water, but you can't make him drink." Maybe so, but you can give the horse so much salt that it increases thirst. The purpose of this book is to fill you with relational salt, so you will thirst for covenant friendships.

While the concept of "covenant" may be unfamiliar to you, it is a central theme of the Bible. A covenant is an agreement between two people or two groups of people. The covenant includes reciprocal promises, and it seals the two parties in a permanent union.

There are many examples of covenants that God made with people in the Bible, including Noah (Genesis 9:1–17), Abraham (Genesis 12:1–3), Moses and the Hebrew people (Exodus 19:3–8; 24:4, 8), and David (2 Samuel 7:12–13). The New Testament is built around a new covenant God made with a broader community, sealed by the blood of Jesus on the cross (Jeremiah 31:31–34; Matthew 26:28; Luke 22:20; 1 Corinthians 11:25; Hebrews 8:9–12; 10:16–17; 12:24). Rather than focusing on covenants that God makes with humans, this book centers on covenants that people make with other people. Covenant friendships are the deepest possible human ties.

The idea of having a covenant relationship with a person to whom we are not married has little purchase in contemporary society. But in my boyhood it was a common concept. Few, if any, of the American covenantal societies, including college fraternities and sororities, are growing. The only fraternal organizations that are growing today are gangs. Culturally we are a society of loners.

Several chapters of the book are devoted to developing and maintaining egalitarian friendships. In these relationships, we are attracted both to the good in ourselves we see mirrored in the other person and to the presence of the risen Christ we sense when we are together (Matthew 18:20; 28:20).

I am not saying covenant friendships are exclusive to the Judeo-Christian tradition. Illustrations of deeply committed relationships, representing every possible religious tradition, abound in history. Aelred, the medieval British abbot of Rievaulx, emphasized that spiritual friendship can be present as long as it is not born of a desire for sexual or temporal advantage.[1]

It is my hope and expectation, therefore, that non-Christians will find this book useful. Nevertheless, a special emphasis has been placed on Christ-aided friendships. I believe that when two people are "held together" (Colossians 1:17) in friendship through the indwelling Christ (John 14:17; Colossians 1:27), a sense of oneness occurs that is as near to heaven as we can experience in this world.

Chapter 8 of this book is devoted to the painful work of terminating friendships. Unfortunately there are times when friendships come to an end. Even Jesus terminated a relationship with one of his closest friends, Judas Iscariot (Matthew 26:47–50). Friendships are like investments: It is important to recognize how to enter them and how to exit them.

The final chapter of the book, Chapter 9: You've Got a Friend, examines a primary friendship—our friendship with Jesus Christ. We will look carefully at how Jesus interacted with his dearest friends, reflect on how his example should affect our friendships, and explore how to cultivate a friendship with Jesus today.

I have made every effort to acknowledge the sources I used in writing this book. If I have unconsciously absorbed the ideas of others, made them my own, and not noted it, I apologize.

Someone said, "Originality is the art of remembering great ideas and forgetting where they came from." (Did someone else actually say that or did I make it up?) Yet many of the ideas expressed in this book are my own. They have come from many years of careful observation and practical experience.

In addition to a generous number of Bible quotations, the reader will note numerous references to the Apocrypha, specifically from the Wisdom of Sirach. The Apocrypha is a collection of Jewish holy books written in the 400-year era between the last book in the Hebrew Bible (the Old Testament) and the first book in the New Testament. I have quoted from Sirach because it has a special interest in relationships.

You will notice numerous references to Alcoholics Anonymous (AA) sprinkled throughout the book. The reason will become apparent in Chapter 1: I am an alcoholic. Even through I have been in recovery for many years, I still go to AA meetings regularly. I gave up anonymity many years ago in the hope that being on the record about my struggles would create space for other strugglers to come out of hiding. AA has taught me that Jesus is the face of our invisible God, that failure is a prerequisite to understanding God's love and grace toward us, and that God's capacity to forgive is greater than ours to sin (Romans 5:20).

The core content of this book was preached in the fall of 2011 at Chapelwood United Methodist Church in Houston, Texas. I was privileged to serve as the senior pastor of this great church from 1994 until I retired in 2014. Those who heard the sermons will recognize significant additions in these pages. There is a time restraint associated with sermons that is not related to a manuscript. Writing the manuscript gave me the liberty to expand my thoughts.

All books remain unfinished, as does life. This book is a work in progress. The manuscript covers my friendship journey up to the time the book went to the publisher.

I close this introduction with poetic words from the pastor of my youth, A. Jason Shirah:

Friendship is a treasure known best
To those who have been welded by its fires
And tempered by its adjustments.
Opposites in relationship
Compensate for deficiencies in each.
Trustworthiness rooted in mutual concern
And affection sustains in times of crisis
Those too sorrowful and weak to stand alone.
Harmony is born in diversity,
And in its fusion of thought and character
Each becomes the person
That going it alone could nevertheless achieve.

Drink the full cup of friendship joy. [2]

Jim Jackson

CHAPTER 1

The Loner's Plight

"The journey of friendship is essential
for the wholeness God intended for us."

Jim Jackson

My friendship journey began abruptly. I was in my early thirties. A church lay leader brought me up short. He looked straight at me and said, "Why do you keep saying, 'My friend this' or 'My friend that'? You do not have any friends! You don't even understand the concept. You do not let anyone get close enough to you to be your friend. You are as alone as anyone I have ever known." That man became my first covenant friend.

But I'm getting ahead of myself. Let me begin at the beginning.

F. Scott Fitzgerald is reported to have said, "What people are ashamed of usually makes a good story." If shame sets the bar, this is going to be an interesting story. I take no pride in telling it. But you are not likely to understand why friendship is such a vital topic to me apart from a few vignettes from my early life. If I have a credential for writing this book, it is my personal struggle.

The fact that I can recount this story now is a miracle. For many years, it was dark and secretive—I did not understand it myself. The price of coming to terms with the past has been thousands of hours of reflection. *New York Times* editorial writer David Brooks says a person is not an expert in a subject area or discipline until he or she has spent ten thousand hours honing the craft. If Brooks is right, then I am an expert in Jim Jackson.

Jim, the Loner

One of my earliest memories is of feeling alone. I was five years old, standing in the front yard of our home in College Station, Texas, playing with a favorite toy—a military tank that fired a plastic projectile. Suddenly it occurred to me that I was a separate person from all the people around me. No one else could see what I saw or feel what I felt. I was alone in the world. This new thought overwhelmed me. Terror bubbled up from the pit of my being. I started crying and ran to my mother for comfort. She asked what had upset me. I was unable to explain, but I never forgot that moment.

Wrapped on both sides of that experience are multiple memories related to my father. Unfortunately, few of these memories are positive. Most of them center on him being impatient or frustrated with me. The message I received from him was that I was not the son he wanted—that I was a disappointment to him. I am sure that I misinterpreted these events in my limited childhood perspective. Children are keen observers but poor interpreters. But it took me another twenty-five years to come to this truth. That means that for twenty-five years, these painful memories were frozen in time with very little objective processing. They became the window through which I looked at my father and myself. For twenty-five years, I lived as though my interpretation of these events was accurate—that

I was a shameful disappointment, and so I had to find a way to keep this truth hidden and to prove my father wrong.

My father died in Cedar Bayou, Texas, when I was six years old. His premature death not only shut the door on our relationship, but it also upended our family's financial security. The photos taken on the day of my father's funeral were telling. Confusion and terror were tattooed to my face. I was not only alone and defective, but I was part of a family that was financially vulnerable.

As a young boy, I tried my best to help our family financially. I have had some kind of job since I was seven years old. I mowed lawns, worked in people's gardens, and sold everything imaginable: Christmas cards, *Grit* newspapers, magazines, gift items—you name it. If you were a neighbor of mine, you were in trouble! The best way to get rid of me was to move! I realize today that I felt far too much financial responsibility for a child my age.

At the same time I wanted desperately to fit in to my environment. To accomplish this feat I fashioned multiple masks, one for every situation. As the years passed, I added new masks to the total, and I got better at wearing them. Many of the masks represented opposite character types—compliant and rebellious, adventurous and cautious, brave and fearful. As I went from one situation to another, I changed masks. It was like having multiple personality disorder, except that I realized that none of the people I was portraying was the real me. The real me was a weak, shameful person. I felt like an actor playing different characters in the same play.

Usually my self-preservation instincts kept people from seeing the real me. But occasionally I did not get the right mask on in time, or I wore an inappropriate mask by accident. In an unguarded moment, something vulnerable leaked out of me. I quickly put on the appropriate mask and hoped people would assume that what they saw or heard was only a momentary inconsistency.

I realize now that I was not the only one around me wearing a mask. Psychologists say it is normal to develop at least two false selves as we pass through adolescence—a public self and a private self. Ordinarily our public selves take one of two shapes: the better-than-I-am mask and the worse-than-I-am mask.

Young people who wear better-than-I-am masks seek to please the authority figures in their lives: parents, teachers, coaches, mentors. They become people-pleasers. Those who wear worse-than-I-am masks do so because they consider it impossible to please the authority figures, so why try? They end up being authority-resisters and peer-pleasers.

These two sets of mask-wearers seem quite different, but they are essentially the same. Both categories are responding to an external audience. The problem with living on the basis of external authority is that it guarantees we will suffer from three disabilities:

- Anxiety. What if people see through my facade and reject me?
- Inability to love and be loved. How can a false self ever love or be loved?
- Incapacity for intimacy. How can a mask-wearer be intimate with another person?

Our family moved multiple times before I graduated from high school. After relocating from Texas to Georgia, we lived in three small south Georgia towns. Changing towns taught me how to adjust to new social situations quickly. Each time, I appeared to fit in well, but I always felt like an outsider. The people I wanted to be friends with were already in a group. They acted like they liked me, but they didn't have additional space in their life for me. I was like a backup player on an athletic team. There were people available for friendship, but they were mostly folks on the social fringes. So I chose to walk alone.

Eventually I became good at walking alone. Truth be told, I preferred it. Aloneness felt safer than closeness. As long as I was alone there was no threat of exposure. I began to define myself as a loner.

My family of origin reinforced that being a loner was acceptable. I cannot remember ever being encouraged to bring a friend home to play or to spend the night. I don't think I even asked for the privilege. I assumed that this sort of behavior just didn't happen in my family.

The Downward Spiral

The casual observer would never have guessed that I lived in self-imposed aloneness. On the outside, there was abundant evidence to the contrary. For example, during the last twenty-seven months of my high school years, we lived in Moultrie, Georgia. I dated a beautiful girl, served as the president of an organization, and was elected captain of an athletic team. On the outside, I looked homogenous with my surroundings. But on the inside, I was suffering from what the folks in Alcoholics Anonymous call "terminal differentness."

In college, things went from bad to worse. Again, I looked pretty good on the surface. I was an athlete, had a girlfriend, and was part of a fraternity. I appeared to have the world by the tail. But on the inside, there was chaos. Predictably it was not long before my life on the surface began to mirror the chaos within me.

Geologists say sinkholes occur when underground water from aquifers is drained. The ground loses its support and caves in. Anything that happens to be on the surface when this natural disaster occurs suddenly sinks. I began to experience sinkholes in my life. I lacked the inner resources to bear the self-imposed pressure being exerted on the surface of my life. So things on the surface began to collapse. I started having emotional, moral, relational, and spiritual sinkholes.

Binge drinking dominated my college life. I not only consumed liquor, but I also sold it—the variety that the government had not bonded or taxed. It never occurred to me that I could go to federal prison for selling moonshine! But even if it had occurred to me, I probably still would have sold it. It was a means to the end I wanted—subsidized booze, side income, and social desirability. I was blind to consequences.

My excessive drinking makes sense to me today. I drank because I was in pain, and alcohol is a painkiller.

The Cycle of Addiction

Here's how the cycle of addition works:

First, people are in pain—deep, psychic pain. I call it "original pain."

Second, they turn to an addictive agent for relief. They need something powerful to kill the pain. There are many alternative drugs of choice—alcohol, pain medication, illegal drugs, sex, work, gambling, food—take your choice. They use whatever it takes to not feel what they are feeling.

Third, the painkiller works. They feel better, freer, more like the self they would rather be.

Fourth, the effects of the addictive agent wear off, and the person feels ashamed of having lost control. The demons in their gut tell them they are a weak, worthless person. Addictions decimate self-esteem.

Fifth, they are now back in their pain, turning again to the addictive agent for relief. The cycle repeats itself—again and again.

Alcoholics Anonymous refer to addictions as "having a friendship without a friend." I was having an intimate friendship with alcohol.

Next, my moral behavior fell into the sinkhole. I did things that were ethically reprehensible. Periodically I am awakened in the night by the memories of things I did as a young man. They appear on the screen on my mind as a horrifying instant replay, disrupting my sleep. I think, Could that have been me? Did I do such a despicable deed? I soon realize it was indeed me. If I did not believe in the undeserved forgiveness and grace of God, I would probably remain sleepless and inconsolable throughout these nights.

Then, the thin vestige of spirituality I absorbed from my mother fell into the sinkhole. I become a militant atheist. The difference between an agnostic and an atheist in my mind is that an atheist is angry about it. And I was angry—very angry. I was convinced that Western Christianity was more cultural than religious. Church membership was a card of admission into middle-class acceptability. I reasoned that if American church members had grown up in India, they would be Hindu; if they had been reared in Saudi Arabia, they would be Muslim. I insisted that what Christians called miracles were actually magic—a combination of sleight of hand and misdirection. I agreed with Sigmund Freud that what people call "God the Father" is a wish projection of an idealized father. Humans, I insisted, invented religion because they could not come to terms with their aloneness, their helplessness, and their mortality. I told everyone who would listen that they were alone in the world, there was no God to rescue them, and at the end of this life there was nothing.

Being an atheist is difficult. The Bible says, "Fools say in their heart, 'There is no God'" (Psalm 14:1). To the psalmist, a "fool" was a morally foolish person. So atheism follows immorality. But it can work the opposite way as well. Atheism can precede immorality. After all, if everything adds up to zero at the end of life, why bother being moral? During this era, I had fleeting thoughts of suicide. If life is painful, why not commit suicide and escape the misery? I looked into the darkness of this abyss for several years.

In an effort to fill the hole in my heart, I flirted with Zen Buddhism. Zen was attractive because adherents did not have to believe in God. But I had a hard time with meditation. The storm inside my heart made it hard to still my body.

I even tried changing colleges. In AA, they call what I did a "geographical cure." And it didn't work. It rarely does. Our problems move with us.

I had a sense that the foundations under my life were disintegrating, but never would have admitted it. I hoped that I was only passing through a bad era and that if I kept my problems hidden, they would improve. In AA, they call that "denial."

There appeared to be two exceptions to my downward spiral. The first was my ability to make money. When I was still in college, I got involved in a business venture and made enough money to drop my basketball scholarship. For my age, I was an enormous success. Suddenly my weaknesses—fear and false identities—became big assets. Fear put its feet in my back and pushed me to compete and achieve. And wearing masks turned me into a master manipulator. Rather than resolving my internal problems, business amplified them. So making money was not really an exception to my downward spiral; it only appeared to be.

The second thing that seemed to go right for me was Susan. I met her toward the end of my college life. When I saw her, I decided that if she were a Jew, I was going to eat kosher for the rest of my life! It was more than her beauty that attracted me. I was drawn to her transparency and authenticity. When you are a fake, you can tell whether other people are genuine. She did not like smoking, so I quit—cold-turkey. I loved her and told her so. To my amazement, she said she loved me and saw great potential in me. Her love frightened me. I feared that she did not love the real me but the person she thought I was. So I decided to tell her about my shadow side. It was my first attempt at coming out of hiding, and I told her things I had never told anyone. No, it was not full disclosure. I told her as much as I thought she could handle. After all, I didn't want to lose her. Within a year, we got married.

I nearly destroyed our marriage that first year. Susan wondered what she had gotten herself into! There were two sources of our problems, and both belonged to me. First, I was trying to do friendship for the first time, and I did not know how. Friendship is the foundation of marriage. People who have never attempted covenant friendship are not good candidates for covenant marriage. Second, I was not an integrated person; I wore multiple masks. The fact that Susan and I have been married since 1967 is nothing short of a miracle. Our survival as a couple is due to the grace of God and Susan's enduring patience.

Conversion: The Beginning of Transformation

The snowballing effects of episodic binge drinking, hating the person I had become, and the realization that I was singlehandedly ruining my marriage finally buckled my knees. I had a genuine conversion experience. While out for an afternoon walk, I passed a small Lutheran church that was open but empty. I sat on the second row on the left side and began to reflect about my life. I saw clearly the mess I had made of things. As I sat there, I began to pray—my first attempt at connecting with the Almighty in a long time. I remember my prayer verbatim, but it had some words in it that don't bear repeating. I have had evangelical colleagues tell me that my prayer was not a "proper" salvation prayer. The one thing I got right was the surrender part of the prayer. I ran up the white flag. I turned my will and way over to God. I told God it was okay to strike me dead for my sins. I was more than willing to die since I felt I wasn't worth much. But I could not go on living in pain. Whatever God did for people, I wanted Him to do in me.

Something dead inside me resurrected that afternoon. Peace flooded my soul. And with it came tears. I could not stop crying. The tears embarrassed me. I tried to stop but couldn't. Pain was pouring from my tear ducts.

Years later, after entering Alcoholics Anonymous, I learned that I had done the first three steps.

Twelve Step Program — Steps One–Three

- Step One: We admitted we were powerless, that our lives had become unmanageable.
- Step Two: We came to believe that a power greater than ourselves could restore us to sanity.
- Step Three: We made a decision to turn our wills and our lives over to the care of God as we understood Him. (And the face of God is Jesus of Nazareth; i.e., Colossians 1:15.)[1]

For a while, I thought God had "fixed" me. The message I picked up in the churches of my youth was that if I got saved, God would fix all my flaws. Isn't that what it means to be a "new creation"? Doesn't the "old" pass away and the "new" come? (2 Corinthians 5:17). What else could conversion mean other than a revolutionary inner change brought about by God?

Spiritual conversion is like a third-world coup. When a new government comes to power, it appears that the old regime has disappeared. But it has only gone underground. The old regime is waiting for the new regime to stumble so it can come out of hiding.

Getting saved was a lot like that for me. My former struggles did not disappear. They simply went underground, waiting for an opportunity to rise again.

When the old temptations and habits reemerged, I reasoned that I must have made some sort of spiritual mistake. Maybe I did pray the wrong prayer. During this era, I must have asked Jesus to come into my heart a hundred times! I also rededicated my life to Christ several times. Each time I hoped that the new spiritual surrender would rid me of the old demons.

But I had changed—at least somewhat. I had quit drinking. My cursing was under control. I had started being a better husband. My insistence that Christianity was rooted in magical thinking gave way to an embrace of mystery—belief in things I did not understand and could not explain. I had even gone back to church. But something was still missing.

I made an appointment with my pastor, and I asked him, "Where did you learn all you know about God?"

He told me he had gone to seminary.

So I asked him, "Where is a seminary?"

When he told me there was one in Atlanta, that was all I needed to hear. Susan and I moved to Atlanta. She enrolled in a graduate program, and I became a part-time seminary student while continuing to keep my business prospering. My search was for hidden, missing pieces, not for pastoral training.

Halfway through seminary, Susan and I went to Europe for six months. During the trip, I hoped to discern whether to start an import business or finish seminary and became a pastor. The time away provided the clarity I needed to sense a leading toward the pastorate. I felt drawn to it—called to it.

A congregation I served on weekends while in seminary reinforced my sense of "call." Today the idea of allowing seminary students to serve churches seems foolish, like allowing medical students to do surgery on the weekend. This brief pastoral experience seemed to second the motion of my call.

I left seminary for my first congregation with high hopes. I was sent to a church in Columbus, Georgia, that had been on mission support for twenty-five years and was about to close. I believed that people needed Christ and that if I had a chance to proclaim the gospel every week, people would choose to follow Jesus.

Statistically my first parish was a smashing success. We grew from 33 to 850 members in five years. The problems I encountered in my parish had nothing to do with the church. The problems were inside me. The church grew, but I faltered internally. My ministry did not rely on the Holy Spirit. I was driven by fear and used the same old masks. I still wasn't "fixed."

I identified with the words of the apostle Paul: "Wretched man that I am! Who will rescue me from this body of death?" (Romans 7:24). Sometimes in the ancient world when a person committed murder, the victim's rotting corpse would be tied to the perpetrator—legs to legs, chest to chest, face to face. Paul was saying that the old self that was supposed to be dead was still attached to him. Paul asked, "Who will rescue me from this dead body?" I identified with that image.

I was disappointed in myself for playing the old games on a new turf—pastoral ministry. I found myself wearing masks, manipulating, people-pleasing, and playing church politics. I had not changed. It felt like the stinking corpse of the old Jim was strapped to the new Jim. "Who will rescue me from his dead body?"

Even more painful, I was emotionally alone. Yes, I was still married, but my inability to be intimate made my aloneness even more unbearable.

In order to overcome my relational deficit, I participated in a weekly prayer and share group throughout my first pastorate. We were supposed to talk about what was going on in our lives and pray for one another. But I never allowed my real issues to surface. My sharing was superficial and well guarded. I was more of an observer than a group participant.

Becoming a New Creation: The Transformation Continues

During this era, we relocated to a parish in Ashburn, Georgia. One evening after a church meeting, the board chair and I engaged in an extended conversation. I made an offhand remark about "friends," and he stopped me in mid-sentence: "Why do you keep saying, 'My friend this' or 'My friend that'? You do not have any friends! You don't even understand the concept. You do not let anyone get close enough to you to be your friend. You are as alone as anyone I have ever known."

Like a superhero with X-ray vision, he was able to see behind my masks and defense mechanisms. Like a skillful surgeon, he exposed my carefully guarded secret. I tried throwing him off my scent, but like a bloodhound, he would not let me escape.

That is what real friends do. They are not afraid to tell the emperor that he has no clothes. Friends hold a mirror before us so we are able to see ourselves more clearly, including things we would rather not see. Friends give us insight into ourselves that we would otherwise have no access to.

I had a decision to make: Would I continue to suffer the hell of a predictable, inauthentic self or risk the hope of an unpredictable, authentic self? I opted to risk the hope of an authentic self. As the apostle Paul put it, I decided to "put away falsehood" (Ephesians 4:25).

I asked my church board chair for the gift of friendship. I specifically asked him to help make more of what was hidden within me visible—to myself and to others. For the next few years, he, two other men, and I met weekly for candid self-disclosure and genuine fellowship. Vulnerability in friendship has to be a two-way street. During those years, the four of us came to know and love one another as our authentic selves.

Again, years later after entering AA, I learned that we were making a feeble attempt at doing steps four through twelve of the Twelve Step program.

Twelve Step Program — Steps Four–Twelve

- Step Four: We made a searching and fearless moral inventory of ourselves.
- Step Five: We admitted to God, to ourselves, and to another human being the exact nature of our wrongs.

- Step Six: We were entirely ready to have God remove all these defects of character.
- Step Seven: We humbly asked God to remove our shortcomings.
- Step Eight: We made a list of all persons we had harmed and became willing to make amends to them all.
- Step Nine: We made direct amends to such people wherever possible, except when to do so would injure them or others.
- Step Ten: We continued to take personal inventory and when we were wrong promptly admitted it.
- Step Eleven: We sought through prayer and meditation to improve our conscious contact with God as we understood God, praying only for knowledge of God's will for us and the power to carry that out.
- Step Twelve: Having had a spiritual awakening as the result of these steps, we tried to carry this message to others and to practice these principles in all our affairs.[2]

The Twelve Steps did not originate with AA. They were developed by a Christian group to help new believers have a step-by-step method of living the Christian life. AA adapted and enlarged the work of this group, substituting the phrase "God as we understood God." The strength of the Twelve Steps is that they lead us through a series of transformational surrenders.

One of the tragedies in the contemporary church is that many believers do the equivalent of steps one, two, and three, and the last half of twelve, and think it is the whole of Christianity. I call it "the Christian four-step"—one, two three, twelve . . . one, two, three, twelve. So we never have to deal with our demons! We never have to tell someone with skin on about the demons or to be held accountable. We never have to make amends. We never have to struggle to maintain conscious contact with God. No wonder there are so many spiritually sick people in the church.

Integration of the Head and Heart

During my years in Ashburn, I began to get my head and my heart together. Through experience, I made a profound discovery: We are not able to think ourselves into a new way of behaving; we have to behave ourselves into a new way of thinking. Just because we understand something does not mean we are changed by it. The danger of mere understanding is that it creates the illusion of personal transformation, but it does not deliver the reality of it. Transformation comes from doing actions on an ongoing basis consistent with the behaviors we would like to have. These experiences interrupt our old way of thinking and carve out a new understanding of ourselves. We start to think of ourselves as a person who does the new behavior.

As we met together week after week, I chose to live consistently with the faith I proclaimed. And I allowed my three friends to hold me accountable for shortcomings. We talked about our victories and our failures and continually encouraged one another.

Through my friends in Ashburn, I came to understand what it means to be part of the body of Christ (1 Corinthians 12:1, 4–31). I began to learn that the church is more of an organism than an organization. I realized that I desperately needed other believers so that I might become the person God intended (1 Corinthians 12:21). With my Ashburn friends, I discovered what it means to come out of hiding, to "walk in the light" rather than the "darkness," and thereby to experience genuine fellowship and forgiveness (1 John 1:6–7). My Ashburn friends helped me to find the courage to expose my character flaws, to seek forgiveness and new intention, and to experience the miracle of accepting community and healing (James 5:16).

Through my three Ashburn friends, I was able to affirm that I was a "new creation" (2 Corinthians 5:17) and that I had within me the resource, the Holy Spirit, for continuing transformation.

Here is the breakthrough concept that exploded in my head and heart: Being a new creation does not mean we suddenly become whole. God's new creation comes into being the same way God's original creation was brought into being—one day at a time (Genesis 1:3–5, 6–8, 9–13, 14–19, 20–23, 24–31). The Almighty does not seem any more in a hurry to finish us than God was to complete the creation of our world. God has the rest of our lives, and perhaps even eternity, to finish us. The bottom line is, we didn't get messed up at once, and we are not likely to get straightened out all at once, either.

Paul said that "all of us . . . are being transformed into Christ's image from one degree of glory to another . . . by the Spirit" (2 Corinthians 3:18). And "all of us" includes Jim Jackson! Even though I was only in day two in the new creation process, I was still a new creation.

Gradually I stood on tiptoes to affirm a new hope—that through God's in dwelling Spirit, I had within me the resources necessary for ongoing transformation, and God would bring it about if I continued to step out of darkness and walk in the light within redemptive fellowship (1 John 1:6–7). God's Spirit was at work to form Christ in me (Galatians 4:18). Like a sculptor, the Spirit was chipping away the parts of me that were not like Christ, revealing in me a work of art. Through Christ I had hope of becoming the Jim whom God intended for me to be when I was born (Colossians 1:27). My part of God's renovation project was to collaborate with the Holy Spirit by risking transparency with safe people.

Human intimacy requires rigorous self-honesty and self-disclosure. The word *intimate* comes from the Latin word *intimus*, which means "inmost." When we have an intimate friendship, we have someone in our lives who knows our true essence. Likewise, we see the inmost essence of our friend.

Salvation is not just about going to heaven when we die. It is about wholeness—mentally, physically, relationally, and spiritually. We cannot become whole by ourselves. We need God and one another to undergo true salvation. Why, then, do we go on hiding our inmost selves from God and worthy friendship candidates? It is shame that keeps us from coming out of hiding, and it is shame that prevents us from walking in the freedom God intends for us.

One of my favorite gospel stories is the account of Jesus raising Lazarus from the dead (John 11:38–44). The stone that had covered the tomb for three days was rolled away, and the resuscitated man came out hopping. He was hopping because his body was bound by grave wrappings. The stench of his previously decaying flesh was still on him. Jesus said to those gathered around, "Unbind him and set him free." Like Lazarus, it is not enough for us to be raised to new life—to become new creations. We need to be unbound and set free from the stench of our former life. But we cannot unbind ourselves. That redemptive work requires community.

An Invitation to a Journey

I make no claim to entire sanctification. I haven't arrived. In fact, I have experienced many spiritual failures since my days in Ashburn. But each period of spiritual recession has occurred because I retreated to my former life as a loner. Each of these relapses brought with it the old chaos and sinkholes. The cost of neglecting transparent friendships has been high. The lesson these failures has taught me is that I need an intimate Christian community in order to be the person God created me to be.

I had a dream in the spring of 1988 that I have come to believe was a revelation from God. The dream was too intricate to detail here. It involved odd symbols and reverse meanings. It took several weeks for me to unlock its secrets. God used the dream to say to me in symbols what the Holy Spirit had been whispering to me for a long time: "You have mistakenly defined yourself as a loner. That is a distorted image of your true identity. From now on, define yourself as a relational person—a person with intimate relationships. Now come out of hiding, open up to other people, and enjoy genuine friends. You have nothing to fear. You will never walk alone again." I have been seeking to be obedient to this heavenly vision ever since (Acts 26:19).

The message contained in my dream is as much for the loners reading this book as it is for me. Do not wait for a dream. Take these printed words as God's message to you. You are not a loner anymore! From now on, you have permission to walk away from that distorted image of your identity. You are at liberty to enter into relational intimacy with a select group of safe friends—to know them and to be known by them.

Choosing to be relational when you have hard-wired yourself to be a loner is like going on a distant journey, similar to the one made by Abraham in Genesis. God instructed Abraham to leave Ur of the Chaldeans and set out, without a road map, not knowing where he would end up (Genesis 12:1–3). Travel in ancient times was dangerous. The journey of friendship is much like Abraham's journey. God does not provide us a relational road map. We are not sure where we are going or how we will get there. And the friendship journey is risky. There is no way to make it a safe journey. Like the traveler on the Jericho Road, you can be attacked, wounded, and left for dead (Luke 10:30–37). Even Jesus' friends betrayed him (Matthew 26:50) and denied him (Matthew 26:69–75). There are no guarantees that your friends will not do the same to you. Nevertheless, the journey of friendship is essential for the wholeness God intended for us.

In life, most of us get injured in relationships. If so, we are not likely to be healed apart from relationships. The thing that hurt us has the best chance of healing us.

God is saying to me, and perhaps to you: *It is time to come out of hiding and begin the journey of friendship. Refuse to settle for a life of aloneness. There is nothing to fear; I am with you.* If God is whispering something similar to this in your spirit, I invite you to join me on the journey to covenant friendship.

CHAPTER 2

Loneliness vs. All Rightness

"As soon as we are conscious, we discover loneliness."

C. S. Lewis

Throughout much of my life, I have suffered from loneliness. If someone had asked me if I was lonely, I would have answered with an emphatic, "No, I have lots of friends." Sadly, I would have believed this response was the truth. I was unaware of the loneliness I felt. The most tragic form of deception is self-deception.

However, if someone had framed the question differently— if they had asked, "Do you feel different than other people?" I would have answered, "Yes, I do." I was the only kid in my elementary classes whose family didn't own their own home. Veterans Administration home mortgage loans were plentiful to returning World War II soldiers. I was the only child around who was fatherless. I hated all the father-son events sponsored by my school and church. And I had trouble reading. When I graduated from high school, I tested at the third-grade, sixth-month reading level. I was thirty-five years old before I learned that I was dyslexic. When you add up these three things, you get a young boy who felt profoundly different and absolutely alone.

Feeling different has been the shape of my loneliness during much of my life. It took me years to realize that many of the people around me, especially in my youth, felt just as different and alone as I did. They also had too much pride to admit their struggle with loneliness.

Some people think loneliness is a rare phenomenon suffered by shy and socially awkward people. They think lonely people should just purchase a copy of Dale Carnegie's *How to Win Friends and Influence People* and then go out and meet people! Superficial suggestions like this prove they are unfamiliar with the universality of loneliness.

Loneliness is the inevitable struggle of every human being. It is part of what makes us human. Each of us experiences loneliness to some extent, in some way, at some time. Loneliness is no respecter of persons. It touches people in every strata of society—the young and the old, the rich and the poor, the educated and the illiterate, the famous and the obscure. People who claim never to have felt lonely either lack self-awareness or are emotionally numb.

Psychologist Thomas Wolfe says it better than I am able: "The whole conviction of my life now rests upon the belief that loneliness, far from being a rare and curious phenomenon particular to myself and a few other men, is the central and inevitable fact of human existence."[1] Loneliness is part of our story, whether we are aware of it or not. Until we come to grips with the reality of loneliness, we do not understand why friendships are so vital to us.

While loneliness is a universal human experience, it can be seen more clearly in Western civilization. The ultimate symbol of Western loneliness is pornography, which has become epidemic. Pornography is counterfeit intimacy.

Types of Loneliness

Loneliness takes many shapes. There are at least three types of loneliness worthy of mention: developmental loneliness, environmental loneliness, and existential loneliness.[2]

Developmental Loneliness

Developmental loneliness refers to the inability to develop and maintain healthy, intimate relationships due to some genetic abnormality or early emotional insult. People with developmental loneliness have attachment issues due to no fault of their own. They hunger for social interaction but sometimes choose to live as "psychological hermits."[3] They find it safer to hold people at a safe distance than to risk injury.

Two illustrations will suffice. Fred is a young man who suffers from a genetic chromosomal disorder called fragile X syndrome. He also suffers from related problems—autism, mental retardation, and social anxiety. Fred has meaningful relationships, but he is extremely cautious with new people. If you want to be Fred's friend, you cannot take his relational hesitancy personally. You must be patient and consistent, and you must prove yourself to him over time. But if you are willing to work at it slowly, Fred will prove to be a loyal friend.

Sally suffers from borderline personality disorder. She vacillates quickly between fear and anger, euphoria and despair. She has a shaky sense of identity and is hypersensitive to real and imagined rejection. If you want to be Sally's friend, you must go slowly, prove yourself over time, and avoid saying or doing things that will produce panic.

Developmental loneliness is a fact of life, and there are throngs of people around us who suffer from it. These are precious, worthwhile people. They deserve our understanding, patience, and friendship.

Environmental Loneliness

Environmental loneliness is isolation due to a special situation in our cultural context. There are circumstances that bring out of us feelings of separation, isolation, and alienation. Unfortunately, environmental loneliness is baked into the structure of our society. There is little likelihood that it is going to decrease and every possibility that it will increase. Each of these environmental circumstances is an impediment to human intimacy. Consider five cultural phenomena that are likely to increase loneliness in the future.

First, urbanization breeds environmental loneliness. The growth of cities in the past fifty years has been exponential. When I was a youngster, Houston, the city in which I now live, had fewer than four hundred thousand people. Today Houston's population is more than ten times as large. And Houston is not unique. All over the world, the masses are moving to large cities in search of jobs.

Cities are places where people are lonely together. Alienation, fragmentation, and distrust, therefore, breed in cities. Genesis records that Cain, who killed his brother Abel, built the first city (4:17). Not long after that, the Bible tells the story of another city and the Tower of Babel (Genesis 9:8–17; 11:1–9). French sociologist Jacques Ellul uses the biblical Tower of Babel account to explain the nature of cities.[4] He says cities have always been where people went to get away from God and to control their own destiny. Cities were places where people went to hide— where they chose to be isolated and detached. Ellul's insight fits with the facts. City dwellers today tend not to work, shop, play, or worship in the neighborhoods where they live. They do not know their neighbors' names. The people they pass on interstate highways during work commutes seem more like objects than human beings. Passersby cannot imagine that these people have the same problems they do. And when they meet new people at social gatherings, they think of them as possible clients or networking resources. Urbanization hinders human intimacy.

Second, mobilization causes environmental loneliness. We uproot our families to get ahead—to land higher positions and salaries, to live in better homes and neighborhoods. This creates a society of rootless nomads.

People who know they are not likely to stay long in a place are less likely to invest in lasting friendships. Why should they make long-term relational investments when they know they will be moving on? When we relocate, we say to friends, "We will stay in touch." But emotional distancing sets in quickly. Social scientists tell us that emotional closeness declines dramatically in the absence of face-to-face contact. That means it does not take long to go from being friends to past acquaintances. Soon communication degenerates to an annual Christmas card exchange. Proverbs 27:10 advises, "Better is a neighbor who is nearby than kindred who are far away."

And mobilization makes it more likely for people to mis-evaluate the relationships they have. For example, mobile people often think of their workmates as friends. But when the employment ends, so do the friendships. Don't take my word for it; ask someone who has gone through a layoff or has recently retired. Teammates and playmates usually are not friends, either. Ask the prodigal son. He thought his far-country party buddies were "friends," but when his money ran out, so did their friendship (Luke 15:13–16).

Third, computerization feeds environmental loneliness. People who deal primarily with machines start to act like machines! And it is impossible to have a personal relationship with a machine. Isn't it interesting how the word *friend* has become a verb? We can now "friend" up to five thousand people on Facebook®. Talk about hyper-connectivity! But no one has five thousand real friends. Most of them are pseudo-friends.

The itch that social media scratches is our need to be known and recognized. If we want to increase our social mobility or to let a large group know what is happening in our lives, social media is an excellent tool. Its downside is that it does a better job of adding to the width of our social network than it does the depth. Just because people have a large number of social media "friends" does not mean that they have meaningful relationships. More often than not, they would not know the people with whom they are LinkedIn® on the street.

I am convinced that one day social scientists will prove that overuse of computerized games and online trivia increases the likelihood of social awkwardness. The reason is that so many people spend so much time in isolation, amusing themselves. The origin of the word *amuse* is literally "not to think."

The same could be said about communication devices. I regularly see people sitting in clusters hiding behind smart phones. Sometimes they are texting the people sitting beside them! They remind me of islands floating beside one another in the ocean—geographically close, even communicating, yet with computerized barriers separating them.

Fourth, singularization can add to environmental loneliness. When Thomas Aquinas wrote the theology of the church in the thirteenth century, he offered people two lifestyle sacraments: marriage or holy orders. It never occurred to him that people without holy orders would choose to stay single. But they are—in increasing numbers.

People are waiting longer to marry. The age of the average "never been married" person whose wedding I perform is almost thirty-two years of age. Early in my ministry, the average was closer to twenty-four. Many people in cities are waiting until their thirties, forties, and even fifties to marry. I have even married first-timers in their sixties!

Many people, especially professional city-dwellers, are choosing not to marry. They remain unattached, choosing either to live with "uncommitted love" (a long-term relationship but not a marriage) or "unconsummated love" (no long-term relationship).[5] Then there are the multitude of the divorcés who would never consider remarriage. Having taken the fragments of their broken dreams up the courthouse steps once was more than enough. Yet these single people, like everyone else, need intentional, intimate friendship.

Fifth, individualization causes environmental loneliness. Ronald Rolheiser offers these powerful words: "The primary philosophical and spiritual problem in the West is the lie of individualism. Individualism makes . . . community almost impossible."[6] Rugged individualism, which is prevalent in American culture, tells us to keep up the appearance, never let them see us sweat, and give people the impression that we have our act together. Hanging out with rugged individualists makes us feel even more lonely.

Paul Wadell carries this idea even further: "We live in a society that teaches us to put ourselves and our needs before the needs and the well-being of others."[7] Individualism prizes personal rights and privileges over the needs of others. The teachings of Jesus fly in the face of individualism. Jesus required us to sublimate our individual wishes and desires in order to consider what is best for others (Mark 8:34–35). The gospel asks us to think of others before we think about ourselves (Philippians 2:3–4).

Western individualism is aided and abetted by materialism. People obsessed with wanting more and more begin to think less and less of others. This has had a debilitating effect on the church. An increasing number of people participate in churches as unaffiliated consumers, taking benefits but being unwilling to commit to communal life. Sociologists call them "Nones." They are the ones who, when asked by the census takers for their religious affiliation, answer, "None."

Individualism leads to fragmentation. We isolate into individual cells rather than being drawn into friendship and corporate life.

Just think about the multiplication of television in modern homes. I was seven years old before our family owned a television. There were family discussions about what to watch, and we had to take turns. But today there is a television in nearly every room of the house, so no one has to take turns. Everyone has the ability to cocoon alone and watch whatever he or she wants. Thus family unity is shattered and a me-first spirit is fostered.

The multiplication of televisions pales in comparison to the growth of smartphones and electronic tablets. Just imagine the long-term effects these tools will have on individualization.

The people who have become absorbed in cultural individualism, and along with it materialism, are poor candidates for covenant friendship or Christian community. They are isolationists and loners.

Do you see that the cultural situation in which we find ourselves is not conducive to intimacy? Urbanization, mobilization, computerization, singularization, and individualization have created an environment where shallow relationships are the norm. Our society resembles a large forest of trees with shallow root systems. We look healthy from a distance, but when the storms of life surge, we are easily uprooted and destroyed.

Existential Loneliness

The most universal form of loneliness is existential loneliness. Existentialism ordinarily refers to a twentieth-century philosophy of hopeless atheism espoused by writers like Jean-Paul Sartre and Albert Camus. According to existentialism, we live in this world due to no decision of our own, yet we are forced to stay here as cosmic orphans. Life is hell, and there is no exit.

I am using the word *existential* in a different sense of the word. "Existential loneliness" is the true nature of our existence whether we are alone or in a crowd. It is an inevitable fact of life. C. S. Lewis wrote, "As soon as we are conscious, we discover loneliness."[8] Ronald Rolheiser put it another way: "No person has ever walked our earth and been free from the pains of loneliness . . . To be human is to be lonely."[9]

King David understood existential loneliness. He wrote, "I am like an owl of the wilderness. I am like a lonely bird on the housetop" (Psalm 102:6). In other words, "I am completely alone. No one feels what I feel."

There were times when Jesus of Nazareth knew this same ultimate aloneness. He cried out from the cross, "My God, my God, why have you forsaken me?" (Matthew 27:46; Mark 15:34).

Unfortunately, existential loneliness is not abated by family gatherings. Many a person can testify that such activities reinforce their feelings of loneliness. Family holiday get-togethers can be painful reminders that we are alone.

Let this truth sink in: We are alone. The issue is not that we *feel* alone. It is that we ARE alone. We came into this world alone. No matter how many people surround us or how close we are to other people, we remain separate from them. And we will die alone. We are existentially alone.

Solutions to Loneliness

We try all manner of things to keep from feeling the pain of loneliness. We run from this pain through frantic activity and perpetual noise. We are busy and loud because we fear the pain that will bubble up from our beings and pierce our conscious minds.

Some numb the pain by indulging in an addictive agent. I have already talked about how people develop addictive disorders to ease their pain. Addictive agents are painkillers. But what is the source of the deep, psychic pain that people seek to anesthetize? It is existential loneliness. For example, why do so many people become sexually obsessed? The answer is simple: People feel lonely and crave intimacy, so they delude themselves into thinking the person in the magazine, on the computer screen, or in a strip club will provide it for them. What they end up with is a blend of self-love and sexual abuse. Wrong thinking acted upon regularly becomes a habit, then an addiction. All addictive disorders are rooted in existential loneliness.

Still others seek to resolve their loneliness by wallowing in the pain. They feel sorry for themselves because of what happened to them in the past or because of the circumstance in which they find themselves. They sponsor an ongoing pity party. But self-pity doesn't help. It creates an inverted rage that feeds off itself and ultimately implodes inside us. Rather than solving the problem, self-pity buries us in anger and depression.

Cultivate Authentic Human Friendships

There is little hope for resolving the issue of loneliness until we face it honestly and work constructively to resolve it. I know of only two things we can do to help us deal with our loneliness.

First, we can cultivate authentic friendships. Sociologists Nicholas A. Christakis and James H. Fowler observed, "Feelings of loneliness arise from the discrepancy between our desire for social connection and our actual social connection."[10] Notice the paradox. Having a good friend decreases loneliness. But when you are lonely, you are less likely to be successful at finding friends and more likely to lose them. "Loneliness," wrote Christakis and Fowler, "is both a cause and a consequence of being disconnected."[11]

Relationships are paradoxical. One can be surrounded by a crowd and still feel alone. Sometimes we are more likely to feel lonely when we are with people than when we are alone. We have all been in crowded places where, in spite of the laughter and frivolity, loneliness hung around us like a dense fog. Some of the most lonely hours of my life have been spent in places surrounded by people.

Likewise, the people who appear to have the most friends, who treat everyone as a long-lost cousin, are often the worst at cultivating deep friendships. They brag about having an abundance of friends, but all of them are chums, colleagues, or comrades. None of them are real friends. These people are cooperative and interactive with others, but they are emotionally disconnected from them. They do not want the vulnerability or the commitment that goes with friendship. A verse in the Apocrypha describes these people: "Many people will say, 'I am your friend'; but some of them are friends in name only" (Sirach 37:1).

Often our loneliness is a subconscious choice. We choose to be alone because of shame and fear of rejection. We think, "I cannot share my true self with these people. They will regard me as unacceptable and I will be humiliated," so we maroon ourselves on an island of aloneness to protect ourselves.

We fear intimate friendship—for good reason. Friendships can be painful. But is that a reason to withdraw from friendships? Few of us would follow this example in any other aspect of our lives. Would we stop playing golf because we had a poor day on the course, or withdraw from school because we did poorly on a test, or withdraw from a sales job because we had a poor month? Of course not. Our choices in life are never between the pain of risking intimacy and no pain. Our choice is between the pain of risking intimacy and the pain of aloneness. The pain of risking intimacy is a far better choice. We are not rocks or islands. We are human beings. And humans need authentic friendship, even though it sometimes causes pain.

In "Choruses from the Rock," T. S. Eliot asked the right question: "What life have you if you have not life together? There is no life that is not lived in community."[12] The contemporary word for this kind of covenant togetherness is communality—a spirit of belonging and cooperation, which arises from a shared commitment to the relationship.

Each of us was designed by God to be relational, to connect with other people. In the creation story, God said, "It is not good for humans to be alone" (Genesis 2:18). We all yearn for someone to know us completely and to love us unconditionally. We are not whole without committed community.

Much of the psychoses people suffer from are rooted in loneliness. Criminal justice experts say that the harshest punishment that can be imposed is solitary confinement. The reason is that it cuts people off from human contact. Penal solitary causes delusional thinking. People who are denied meaningful contact with other people lose touch with reality.

Likewise, much of our neuroses are rooted in friendlessness. Several years ago, while traveling in Egypt, I met a famous Arab psychiatrist. He told me that his practice centered exclusively on psychosis, because neuroses were virtually nonexistent in the Middle East. I will never forget his words: "Neurosis grows in environments where there is a lack of community. When people have no one with whom to talk about their burdens and fears, they become neurotic. Neurosis is a problem in your country because most Americans do not have friends."

Several years ago, William Schofield wrote a book called *Psychotherapy: The Purchase of Friendship*. The thesis of his book is that because people have no trustworthy, confidential friend with whom they can unburden themselves emotionally, they pay professionals to listen to them. Many times, the people in psychotherapy would be as well served by a friend or a Twelve Step group that offers caring, compassion, and wisdom. They do not know where to find this, and so they pay someone to provide it for them. It is possible that Schofield overstates the case, but his comments call for serious reflection. Ask lawyers, doctors, waiters, cosmetologists, barbers, bartenders, or clergy—they will tell you they often play the role of surrogate therapist. People will unburden themselves to anyone who they think might listen sympathetically and not repeat the story to others. The over-dependence on professionals makes it less likely that people will seek the kind of relationships they really need—true friendships.

I cannot tell you how many times I have been listening to people tell their stories, and when they finished, asked them, "How many people other than me know this story?" Over and over, I have heard the same response: "No one." Occasionally I will ask a follow-up question: "How does it feel to be alone—to be friendless?"

Why would Christians choose to live in friendless isolation? None of us can make it alone in this world. If we get singled out in life, we get picked off. After all, are we not the body of Christ? (1 Corinthians 12:12–27). Are we not the means by which Christ is made visible to the world? Jesus of Nazareth is no longer present on the stage of history, but he remains present through his incarnation, the church. When we encounter one of Christ's followers, we are experiencing something sacramental—the spiritual through the natural, the invisible through the visible.

Through Christ, we literally belong to one another. We are the body of Christ. Believers should be closer to one another than we are to our biological siblings. Our closeness should be a manifestation of Christ's life in us (1 John 4:11–12, 20–21). Because we share a common life in the Lord Jesus, we are able to live in transparent community (Acts 2:44; 4:32). The church is to be a community of friends (3 John 15).

Yet every time we go to church, we are surrounded by lonely people. These people look as if they are self-sufficient, but they are not. They have the same relational needs and longings we have. When will we learn to risk saying, "I need you"? It takes courage to ask another person for the gift of friendship. They could ignore us, reject us, or humiliate us. But is it not better to risk failing at intimacy than to continue living in self-imposed isolation? Is it not more honest to hazard rebuff than to go on pretending a lie—that we are "fine, thanks"?

Jesus told his apostles he needed them. He called them "to be with him" (Mark 3:14). During his last Passover meal with the apostles, Jesus washed their feet. In order to do that, scripture says he "laid aside his outward garment" (John 13:4). This means that as he washed the apostles' feet, all Jesus had on was his inner garment—the nightgown one exposed only to family at bedtime. The robe Jesus removed was how most people recognized him. It represented his outward identity. What an amazing demonstration of intimacy!

Paul was not ashamed to admit his relational needs. He called out to friends and asked them to travel a long distance to help him prepare to die (2 Timothy 4:9–16). We, too, must learn to overcome our relational reluctance.

Solomon gave us sound advice about cultivating friendships: "Two are better than one" (Ecclesiastes 4:9). Here is a paraphrase of Solomon's four reasons friendship is vitally important (Ecclesiastes 4:9–12):

1. Because there is greater synergy with two people working together than with two people working independently.
2. Because sooner or later, we are going to fall, and we will need someone to pick us up.
3. Because life tends to be cold and impersonal, and human relationships restore warmth to our lives.
4. Because one day we will be attacked, and we will need someone to stand beside us.

Are these not good reasons to work at authentic friendship connections?

When I think of the kind of intimacy Ecclesiastes 4:9–12 describes, the picture of two people living in a duplex apartment comes to mind. They share a front porch, but each has his own apartment. Occasionally the two people sit together on the front porch and talk. As time passes, they invite each other into their front rooms. But they have not explored all their own back rooms. As they make this exploration, they share with their friend what they have discovered in the new rooms. They allow their neighbor to see their duplex, even if it is messy. Eventually each person knows the other person's side of the duplex as well as they know their own. They live side-by-side in intimacy. They know one another's unkempt souls. God's goal for our relational journey involves continually expanding the boundaries of self-knowledge and sharing what we have learned with friends.

People often mistakenly believe that detachment gives them emotional independence and protection against relational entanglement. We should be involved with others, but not too much. We should measure our relational investments the way one reserves something of great value that is in short supply. But the result is the pain of isolation. The price is too great! It is better to manage the dangers of enmeshment than to be devoid of meaningful relationships.

When we choose to reach out to another person in friendship, we cast a fragile bridge across the chasm of our solitude and invite another person to cross over. As a result, we are no longer as alone. If we have one real friend, we will never be completely alone.

Cultivate Divine Companionship

A second suggestion to help eliminate our sense of loneliness is to cultivate divine companionship. Blaise Pascal wrote, "All human problems stem from man's inability to sit quietly in a room alone."[13] In other words, the solution to our problems is to be able to sit quietly without being driven to speak or act. What a true and powerful statement! It is our inner emptiness that drives us to be compulsive—to say things that we do not need to say and to do things we do not need to do. None of the things we crave can fill the void within us, not even human companionship! Only God can provide the presence and peace we seek. Only God knows what we see and feel, and, therefore, only God can be with us in our ultimate aloneness. However, in order to experience God's gift of friendship, we must be willing to sit quietly in a room with God.

Earlier in this chapter, I wrote about existential loneliness being a common human experience. Whether we are aware of it or not, each of us has a primal longing. And behind this inner ache is a yearning for God—homesickness for the divine. Often we do not recognize it as such. It just feels as if something is missing. Ronald Rolheiser says, "Our is really nothing other than our to thirst and restlessness to return to God."[14] It is what a homing instinct is for pigeons. God gave us this spiritual instinct to lead us back to our original habitat. And what is that habitat? Paul said, "We live and move and have our being" in God (Acts 17:28). This primal longing is what the prodigal son felt when he came to himself and said, "I will get up and go to my father" (Luke 15:18).

The greatest proof of God's existence is the longing we feel when we do not sense God's companionship. God is the only one who can satisfy this inner hunger. Why? Because God created the hunger. Augustine long ago wrote, "You have made us for yourself, and our heart is restless until it rests in you."[15]

The crass materialism of Western culture is about trying to fill this emptiness with things. We collect trinkets of wealth and possessions in order to feel secure and fill the voids in our souls. But what we hunger for is God's presence and peace. When we finally arrive there, we sense that we are back where we started—in the place where we belong—in the garden of Eden. The more we try to fill our souls with things, the farther from home we roam and the more restless we become.

How do we cultivate God's companionship and return to our true home? Let me offer two simple suggestions:

First, have a genuine desire for a relationship with God. Nicholas A. Christakis and James H. Fowler agree that our relationship with God affects our social network.[20] The means God has provided for us to attain this relationship is prayer. Prayer is how we respond to the deepest cries of our hearts. The psalmist says, "As a deer longs for flowing streams, so my soul longs for you, O God. My soul thirsts for God, for the living God" (42:1–2). And if we want a relationship with God, we can have one. Scripture teaches, "If you search for God with all your heart and soul, you will find God" (Deuteronomy 4:29; Jeremiah 29:13). James wrote, "Draw near to God and God will draw near to you" (4:8). Jesus said, "Blessed are those who hunger and thirst for spiritual righteousness, for they will be satisfied" (Matthew 5:6).

Second, seek what can be known about God through his Son, Jesus. If we are serious about a relationship with God, we want to know what God is like. How can we know God's character? Is God like nature? Nature is about the survival of the fittest. Do we look solely to our personal experiences to understand God? What if we lack experience or misinterpret our experiences? Is the Almighty limited to our spiritual experiences? We come to know God through Jesus. He is the face of the invisible God. Paul wrote, "In him [Jesus] the fullness of deity was pleased to dwell" (Colossians 2:19). Jesus is Immanuel, "God with us" (Matthew 1:23). When we get to heaven, the God we encounter will be Jesus. If we want to know God, our first step should be toward Jesus of Nazareth.

Take time for solitude with God. Loneliness and solitude are vastly different. Loneliness produces feelings of separation, alienation, and anxiety; solitude bears the fruit of peace. Notice the paradox: The path out of loneliness is solitude with God?

Solitude is about choosing to be alone in a spiritual way—to be alone with God. The only way to have God's enduring peace is to create the necessary space for aloneness with God. Jesus made it clear that without solitude, there can be no intimate communion with God (Matthew 6:6). So without solitude, we can know God only superficially. Solitude is about mindfully creating space for God and choosing to join the Almighty in it. We cannot know God intimately if we fear solitude. This should not surprise us. All relationships, marriage and friendship included, require intentional togetherness. If we want a human relationship to flourish, we have to say "no" to something or somebody so there will be room for the relationship.

Solitude requires courage. It is hard for us to say no to our compulsive busyness and need to be entertained. Likewise, solitude requires faith—faith to believe that God will join us in the space we create (Matthew 28:20) and that the God who shows up will love and accept us.

There are four fundamental things we have to take care of if we want to experience aloneness with God:

1. Having a right time
2. Having a right place
3. Having sufficient quiet
4. Having a willingness to be still

We cannot live consciously without experiencing some form of loneliness. The only question is what resources we will turn to when it arises. God's provisions are covenant friends and companionship with the Creator.

Ecclesiastes 4:9–12 concludes with these words: "A three-fold cord is not quickly broken." Solomon had been pointing out, "Two are better than one," and all of a sudden, at the end of verse 12, he starts talking about the importance of a third party. The third person he is talking about is God, our eternal Friend. Jesus said, "For where two or more are gathered in my name, I am in the midst of them" (Matthew 18:20). When our lives are drawn together with a close friend and the Holy One, we become a three-fold cord. And the events of life, no matter how tragic or severe, are not able to wrench us apart.

Notice that having relationships between God and others is not mutually exclusive. Being alone with God actually improves our relationships with others. It sensitizes us to both our differences and our similarities.

When I focus my attention on the twin priorities of intimate friendship with God and intimate friendship with a few safe people, I have a deep sense of what I call "all-rightness." I have an inner assurance that the three-fold cord will hold.

CHAPTER 3

The Beauty of Covenant Friendship

"Friends are friends forever
when the Lord's the Lord of them."

Michael W. Smith

Several years ago, Susan and I were in Cambridge, Massachusetts, visiting the home of poet Henry Wadsworth Longfellow. An old picture on a table in the foyer made a lasting impression on me. It was a group of scruffy men with beards. I asked our guide who the people were. She called the names of some of America's great literary minds—Longfellow, Ralph Waldo Emerson, Henry David Thoreau, James Russell Lowell, Nathaniel Hawthorne, and John Greenleaf Whittier. The six men called themselves the Saturday Club. They met at Longfellow's house each Saturday to read to one another what they had been writing and to receive mutual encouragement. They were close personal friends. Longfellow, who was the most successful economically, often supported other group members financially when they went through lean times.

I have thought many times about our visit to Longfellow's house. It gave me an important window to look at covenant friendship. Those friends, who shared the same craft, chose to support one another rather than compete. We all need the equivalent of a Saturday Club.

I have often said that a friend is someone who would drive more than five hundred miles to attend your funeral. If my five-hundred-mile rule is the bar for friendship, I have bad news for you: They can all come in one car—a compact car! None of us has many true friends. We may have multiple colleagues and comrades, but few of us have a large number of Saturday Club–level friends.

Many people live like pioneers—isolated, friendless lives. They think of themselves as having many friends, but no one knows their secrets or struggles. They do not have a non-family member who is committed to standing beside them regardless of circumstances. I want to focus this chapter on how to establish Saturday Club–type friendships—or what I call "covenant friendships."

What Is a Covenant?

The term *covenant* is unfamiliar to most of us. If we have heard the term, it has been in relation to two relational rituals: marriage and adoption. Let's consider both of them.

On one hand, a contract is a legal agreement that establishes the terms by which what has been agreed upon will be carried out. It also includes the terms by which the contract can be terminated. Contracts establish the baselines for lawsuits and thus can end.

Covenants, on the other hand, are not intended to be terminated. Covenants are the means by which two people are bonded. Marriage, for example, is a covenant—"the two become one flesh" (Genesis 2:24).

Adoption is another example of a covenant. Paul compared Christian believers to God's adopted children (Romans 8:14–17; Galatians 4:4–7). The Hebrew people were God's natural children (Romans 11:1–32). Gentile believers are related to God through adoption. The relationship between birth parents and adoptive parents to their children is fundamentally different. For example, birth parents were allowed to disown their children, but adoptive parents were not given that right. They chose their children. Therefore, the bond between adopted children and their parents is stronger than the bond between birth children and their parents. According to the birth narrative in Matthew's and Luke's gospels, Joseph was not biologically related to Jesus. Jesus was listed in Joseph's genealogy through the covenant of adoption (Matthew 1:16; Luke 3:23). Likewise, the basis of our assurance that we are in God's family and will remain so has nothing to do with perfect performance. Our assurance is rooted in the covenant of adoption.

The Bible makes an assumption that too few people grasp: Blood relationships are temporary, but covenant relationships are permanent. For example, when our biological children marry, they leave their parents and enter a covenant with someone with whom they have no blood tie (Genesis 2:24). If we hope to have an enduring relationship with our biological family members—children, siblings, or parents—we must be willing to release them. That means refusing to control them or be controlled by them. Only then can friendship with a blood relative have hope of becoming covenantal. When friendship does occur between blood relatives, it means that a profound change has taken place: we are now bound together by covenant rather than blood. Our children, siblings, or parents are now more friends than relatives. We should count ourselves fortunate if family members become friends and friends become family.

One of the best examples of a covenant friendship found in the Bible is Jonathan and David. These two young men were a blend of alike and unlike. Jonathan and David had both proven their mettle in military conflicts. There was physical, intellectual, and moral parity between them. They each saw their match in the other person. Small people are intimidated by and avoid relational equals. But wise people look to their equals for friends. Proverbs 27:17 says, "As iron sharpens iron, so one person sharpens the wits of another."

But the social backgrounds of Jonathan and David could not have been more different. Jonathan was a prince, King Saul's eldest son. David was the youngest son of Jesse, a peasant shepherd. Yet in spite of these differences, a friendship bond emerged. Aristotle would have described their relationship as a "perfect friendship."[1]

There are two passages in the Bible that discuss the covenant between Jonathan and David (1 Samuel 18:1–4 and 23:14–18). These accounts describe their covenant making and covenant renewals.

Making a Covenant

When Jonathan and David established their friendship covenant, Scripture says their souls were "knit together" (1 Samuel 18:1). That word *knit* in Hebrew means "to sew something together in such a way as to make it seamless." It was as if someone super-glued their souls together. Aristotle is reputed to have spoken of friendship as "one soul in two bodies." That is what happened between Jonathan and David. Their friend became their other self.

Unfortunately, Western society sees friendships as more contractual than covenantal. We remain loyal to our relational commitments as long as it is convenient and in our best interest. However, when relationships no longer help us to achieve our goals, the ties that bind us begin to loosen. Soon the relationship is considered expendable; i.e., the demise of marriage in Western civilization. Fewer people are getting married and more married people are getting divorced. The reason is simple: Marriage is viewed as a contract rather than a covenant. Western culture has a shallow grasp of the concept of covenant.

Covenant friendship is not a matter of convenience—we work the same jobs, live in the same neighborhood, go to the same church, remain members of the same club, have children who go to the same school, live in the same town, agree with one another politically, and so forth. True friendship is not a means of achieving self-interests "as long as self-improvement shall last." Covenant friendships are like marriage is supposed to be—for better or for worse; for richer or for poorer; in sickness and in health; as long as you both shall live. Proverbs 27:10 says, "Do not forsake your friend."

Covenant friendship carries with it obligations that go beyond death. As the Bible says, "Love never ends" (1 Corinthians 13:8). Friendship is a bond that neither space nor time can alter.

One of the most moving parts of David's saga occurred after Jonathan's death. David, as king of Israel, asked his servant, "Is there anyone left in the house of Saul to whom I can show kindness for Jonathan's sake?" (2 Samuel 9:1). The servant knew the whereabouts of Mephibosheth, a son of Jonathan. Mephibosheth was unable to walk because both his feet had been injured (2 Samuel 9:3, 13). The poor young man was being kept in hiding, probably because his protectors thought David would see him as a threat to his kingship and kill him. After all, Mephibosheth was King Saul's grandson.

The servant brought Jonathan's son to David. No doubt afraid of the king, Mephibosheth spoke only four words: "I am your servant" (2 Samuel 9:6). In response, David said to him, "Do not be afraid, for I will show you kindness for the sake of your father, Jonathan; I will restore to you all the land of your grandfather, Saul, and you shall eat at my table always" (2 Samuel 9:7). In other words, instead of being treated as an enemy, Mephibosheth was adopted as David's surrogate son (2 Samuel 9:11). Without being asked, David gave to Mephibosheth possessions, position, and prestige he had never earned. And he did it all "for Jonathan's sake" (1 Samuel 9:1, 7). I rarely receive Holy Communion without thinking of the story of Mephibosheth. Why am I privileged to eat at the Lord's table? We are invited to eat at God's table always, for Jesus' sake.

Have you ever been given some advantage you did not earn because of a mutual friendship? Or have you extended an undeserved courtesy to someone for the sake of a friend? If so, you have some understanding of how far the boundaries of friendship extend.

Notice five important things about the friendship covenant between Jonathan and David.

Recognition of Need

First, both Jonathan and David recognized a need for a deeper human tie. Both men were national heroes. Both men had many friends. There is a long list of David's friends in 2 Samuel 23:8–39. Both men, though, were conscious of needing a deeper kind of friendship than they had known previously.

We never make major changes until we are aware that something is missing—that something needs to change. As long as we think we are "getting along just fine, thank you," a situation remains static. Our attitude is, "It ain't broke, so don't fix it." As long as we think our existing friendships are adequate, we are not likely to seek a covenant-level friendship.

Though I claimed to have many friends, there came a season when my need for a deeper level of friendship shouted to me. It was only then that I began to do something about it.

Same Gender vs. Different Gender

The second thing we notice about the friendship covenant between David and Jonathan is that they are both male. They were of the same gender.

There is a profound difference between covenant marriage and covenant friendship. Both are covenant relationships, but covenant marriage is sexual. We sleep with our spouses. We do not sleep with our friends.

I am convinced that one of the relational errors taking place in our culture is that many people are attempting covenant marriage before they have engaged in a covenant friendship. They have therefore not done the hard work of self-integration or faith integration. As I mentioned in the introduction, when these people marry, their spouses soon discover they married different people from the ones they dated. They often feel they have been victim to a "bait and switch." They begin to ask, "What happened to the person with whom I fell in love?" Sometimes both spouses feel this way. A marital crisis develops because they are essentially two false selves trying to live in intimacy. The results of such marriages are poor. I strongly advise people to engage in a covenant friendship before they attempt covenant marriage.

But even if we are engaged in an intimate marriage, it does not negate the need for a covenant friend. There are things we would be better off discussing with a friend than with our spouse. For example, if you are having sexual temptations, why worry your spouse? Talking to a friend and asking the friend to hold you accountable for not crossing the appropriate verbal and physical boundary lines would be far more productive.

Can men and women be friends? Ronald Rolheiser points out a painful fact: "One of the deep wounds in Western culture is that men and women find it hard to be friends. It's easy for them to be lovers, but not friends."[2]

However, Jesus had quite a few platonic, non-carnal, opposite-gender friendships. Luke 8:1–3 points out that Jesus and the disciples traveled with and were financially supported by several married women. Four are mentioned by name in the passage. Think of it: Jesus, the disciples, and a bunch of married women traveling together. And the women were picking up the tab! Jesus also had a close friendship with the two sisters of Lazarus, Mary and Martha (Luke 10:38–42; John 11:1–44). These three people offered Jesus a "safe house" when he was in the Jerusalem area. But we can be sure Jesus was sexually above reproach. We know this because if anyone had been suspicious of sexual impropriety, it would have been mentioned in the text. It was the pattern of the New Testament writers to answer rumors in the biblical text; i.e., Matthew 28:11–15. There must have been something about the way Jesus handled those friendships that assured people that he was sexually chaste.

There are many examples in church history of nonsexual, different-gender friendships:

- John of the Cross and Teresa of Avila
- Francis de Sales and Jane Frances of Chantal
- Vincent de Paul and Louise de Marillac
- Raymond of Capua and Catherine of Siena
- Don Marabotti and Catherine of Genoa
- Francis of Assisi and Clare of Assisi

Different-gender covenant friendship enriched the lives of these saints.

However, most of us are not saints. We have not yet reached the place where godliness and self-restraint have removed sexual temptation from our relational equation. Let's face it; it is hard for a man not to regard a woman as a female, and it is hard for a woman not to regard a man as a male. In these situations, it is easy for us to become confused, especially if we are unconsciously starved for intimacy.

Counselors talk about this confusion in terms of transference and countertransference. Transference is the "subconscious tendency to redirect needs, feelings, desires, and expectations related to some other person to the person at hand." Countertransference is the "subconscious tendency to respond in a reciprocal way." The danger is that both of these happen subconsciously in relationships all the time.

When I was in high school, I was alone with a female friend one night. We were both going steady with someone else. We were just neighbors and friends. But that evening, I suddenly felt the urge to kiss her. As I look back on the experience today, it is clear to me that I felt lonely, cared about her, and did not know what to do with those feelings. Fortunately, I did not kiss her, but I learned that different-gender friendships can be confusing.

If we are not careful, we can speak words that should not have been spoken and cannot be unspoken. Humans are created in the image of God (Genesis 1:26-27). Part of what being in God's image means is that, like God, we speak things into existence (Genesis 1:6, 9, 14, 20, 24, 26). Relationships, including sexual relationships, are brought into being more by words than by any other means. When words are spoken, emotions follow. Then we are tempted to act on our words, and this can easily lead to sexual activity.

Not all mixed-gender friendships are doomed to slide into sexual passion. The human libido notwithstanding, many males and females are able to have successful friendships. Half the human race should not be automatically excluded from our pool of friendship possibilities.

However, because mixed-gender relationships are more dangerous, we should take extra precautions to make sure the relationship does not become sexual. It is preferable for us to choose opposite-gender friends with whom we are not likely to be sexually attracted. It would be wise to practice the twin disciplines of visibility and interrupt ability. Think of all the problems the Roman Catholic Church could have avoided if priests had kept their doors opened and people had been allowed to interrupt them. The Apocrypha advises, "Never dine with another man's wife, or revel with her at wine; or your heart will turn aside to her, and in your spirit you may be plunged into destruction" (Sirach 9:9). There are words that should not be spoken. There are physical boundaries we should not cross. Friendship is also "a time to refrain from embracing" (Ecclesiastes 3:5). Beware of secrecy and deception. If you are married and the friendship starts to make you discontented with your marriage, the friendship should end.

I realize that we live in a culture that accepts casual sex—that it is acceptable to have "friends with benefits"—but this view does not square with reality. Many a wonderful friendship has been ruined by people who crossed the line sexually. When this happens, the relationship shifts from covenant friendship to covenant marriage. The friendship is lost and is unlikely to be restored, even if the sexual relationship is broken off. The genie won't fit back in the bottle. Very few people are able to move from being former lovers back to friendship. If the friendship becomes romantic, we are choosing to end the friendship.

Different Backgrounds

The third element we can observe in the covenant between Jonathan and David is that they were from different socioeconomic backgrounds. David and Jonathan came from opposite sides of the tracks. David came from a poor peasant family; Jonathan was reared in luxury in the palace. But as David and Jonathan came to know each other, they discovered they were cut from the same bolt of cloth.

We need friends who will stretch us—people who have had different life experiences. After all, we live in a culturally diverse world, and we are preparing for an eternity where there will be people from "every tribe and language and people and nation" (Revelation 5:9).

The values of God's kingdom are radically different from the values of this world. Our choice of friends does not have to be limited by people's wealth, education, race, ethnicity, or age. In fact, everyone needs at least one close friend with whom we have little in common. These friendships will help us overcome our natural prejudices.

I once saw a TV show I have never forgotten. Two women, one white and the other black, were placed in a nursing home. They had both had debilitating strokes. One lady was disabled on the right side of her body and the other on her left. Both ladies had played the piano throughout their lives. Every day they sat in the day room of the nursing home grieving that their piano playing days were over. One day a social worker brought the women to the piano and insisted that they play. The case worker realized that if they played together, one using the left hand and the other using the right, they could play any piece of music. That night on the show, the two ladies played "Ebony and Ivory." It was a smash hit.

Another possibility is to make friends with someone who is physically or mentally challenged. The friendship of two women in my church is inspirational. One has used a wheelchair for many years. The other woman does not have any disabilities. Yet there is remarkable equity in the friendship between the two women.

Look for potential covenant friends from backgrounds dissimilar to your own. You may find a remarkable human being worth knowing.

Mutual Attraction

The fourth element in the friendship narrative of Jonathan and David is their attraction to one another. Covenant friendships always have an element of chemistry. We are emotionally attracted to friends for who they are or what they have accomplished. We have common interests, values, and beliefs. There is something about the person's character or personality that catches our attention and makes us want to enjoy their company. Often they bring out the best in us. I like the opening lines of Mary Carolyn Davies's poem "This Is Friendship":

I love you, not only for what you are,
But for what I am when I am with you.
I love you, not only for what you have made of yourself,
But what you are making of me.[3]

The biblical text says Jonathan and David "loved" each other (1 Samuel 18:1, 3). On one occasion they even kissed (1 Samuel 20:41). Two men loving and kissing each other in friendship sounds strange to Western ears. Some revisionist theologians have insisted that the affection between David and Jonathan was homosexual. They point out that David's love for Jonathan "surpassed" his love for women (2 Samuel 1:26). But three thousand years ago, such expressions of affection between friends were common. Cicero, the Roman statesman and orator, said, "What is a friend but a partnership in love."[4]

The farther you go to the East today, the more likely you are to see people of the same gender express their affection publicly. On a trip into East Germany in 1970, I saw a political poster that shocked me. It represented Leonid Brezhnev, the former prime minister of the Soviet Union, kissing Erich Honecker, the former prime minister of East Germany—on the mouth! The poster was intended to show the love and commitment between these two former nations. No one in East Germany at the time thought of the poster as unusual or inappropriate.

Westerners are awkward, hesitant, and inhibited about male contact. Most male touching is somewhere between aggressive and violent. Consider everything from hand-shaking to football.

It is true that there have been times when same-gender affection has crossed the line and become sexual. According to the historian Bryan Patrick McGuire, early in the Middle Ages, the church began to grow concerned about the expression of affection between people who had made holy vows, such as priests, monks, and nuns. Ecclesiastical laws were developed governing various demonstrations of affection: Embracing, holding hands, etc. There was a fear that demonstrative behavior would lead to homosexual love, which was a violation of the vow of celibacy.[5]

Ritual: Words and Deeds

A fifth ingredient included in the covenant Jonathan and David made was ritual. They used a collection of consecrated words and deeds to officially seal their covenant.

1. Words. Jonathan and David made a formal oath of loyalty to one another. They made an irrevocable vow binding them to the relationship. These words branded them deep and forged a lifelong bond between them.

In a covenant friendship, it is important to define the relationship. It helps both parties to know what they can expect from the other person. It is for this reason that I encourage the couples I marry to write their own vows. They need to put what they are promising in their own words. I recommend that covenant friends do the same thing. Define the relationship in your own words. Assumptions are often misunderstandings.

Being in a covenant implies the intentional sacrifice of independence. We voluntarily choose to be less free than we were prior to the commitment. Being in a covenant friendship means we no longer think about what is best for us alone. We think of what is best for us and our friend.

Think of how monumental a covenant with David was for Jonathan. Every day of his life, someone said to him, "One day when you are the king . . . " He didn't grow up wondering what he was going to be when he was grown. He was the prince. That determined what he learned and did, as well as how he thought. Everyone knew Jonathan was destined to be Israel's next king. He was Saul's firstborn son and heir. That meant he had position, prestige, power, and possessions.

Yet through their friendship Jonathan began to see in David the qualities needed for Israel's next king—qualities he did not possess. Jonathan could have seen David as a threat. He could have become jealous, resentful, and bitter. He could have engaged in fault-finding, criticism, and anger. He could have done what his father, King Saul, did—see David's successes as a sign of his failure. Instead he demonstrated unwavering support for his friend over and over:

- He warned David of potential disaster (1 Samuel 19:1).
- He spoke well of David to his father (1 Samuel 19:4).
- He offered to do whatever David wanted him to do (1 Samuel 20:4).
- He devised a plan of escape for David (1 Samuel 20:18–22).
- He maintained confidentiality with David (1 Samuel 20:35–40).

In spite of opposition from his father, King Saul, Jonathan intentionally pursued a relationship with David and entered into a covenant friendship with him. He had everything to lose and nothing to gain. He sacrificed his considerable position because he believed it was God's will for David to be Israel's next king. Jonathan took a posture toward David similar to the one John the Baptist took toward Jesus: "He must increase, but I must decrease" (John 3:30).

2. Deeds. Jonathan and David symbolized their covenant friendship with ritual deeds. People making a covenant have sometimes commingled their blood. I performed this ritual with two friends when I was an adolescent. (Come to think of it, I have not seen or heard from those fellows in over fifty years!

Another deed used to consummate a covenant has been offering a sacrifice and the sharing of a meal. It is easy to see these elements in Holy Communion. The holy meal Jesus shared with his apostles on Thursday evening pointed to the New Covenant (Jeremiah 31:31–34; Hebrews 8:1–12) that he would cut on the cross on Friday—"This is my body. . . This is my blood" (Matthew 26:26–27; Mark 14:22–24; Luke 22:19–20; 1 Corinthians 22:24–25).

In the case of Jonathan and David, they exchanged property. First, they exchanged weaponry. That symbolized they would never be rivals or enemies. Nothing and no one would drive a wedge between them. The principle of non-competition is an important part of covenant making. Competition makes empathy impossible. It promotes isolation and secrecy. Competition kills relationships. You cannot be covenant friends with someone over whom you are trying to gain the upper hand. Real love refuses to play "king of the hill" and chooses instead to play "king maker." The greatest demonstration of friendship is to celebrate the accomplishments of a friend who advances beyond you in honor, reputation, position, or wealth. By exchanging weapons, Jonathan and David said to each other, "Your enemies are my enemies, and your friends are my friends. I have your back." A friend of mine likes to say, "The enemy of my friend is my enemy."

Regarding their weapons, it is interesting to note that only Jonathan had a sword. There were only two swords in all of Israel, one belonging to King Saul and the other belonging to Prince Jonathan (1 Samuel 3:22).

Next, David and Jonathan put on one another's clothing. In those days, a person's clothing was a symbol of their financial assets. Ancient people wore their wealth. By exchanging clothing, David and Jonathan were saying to each other, "What's mine is yours, and what's yours is mine. If you are in trouble, I am in trouble. If you have plenty, I have plenty."

Our culture has only one parallel of this exchange of clothing, and it is related to the covenant of marriage. Couples ordinarily exchange rings during their wedding. When they do that, they are saying to one another, "This ring represents all that I am and all that I have. I give it to you because we are now one. When you look at this ring, remember that what's mine is yours, because I am yours. From this day on, we are one."

Covenant Friendship Rituals

There is historical evidence that the church blessed same-gender covenant friendships until the fifteenth century.[7] These covenant services looked a great deal like a contemporary wedding service. There was an exchange of vows without a ring exchange.[8] The service was often followed by a fellowship meal.[9] These covenant friendship services were ultimately banned by the Western church, and no printed copies of the liturgies remain.[10] However, there are numerous printed copies of the friendship rituals that remain. They are the property of Orthodox churches in Central and Eastern Europe.[11]

According to historians, the ritual of friendship was discontinued for two reasons. First, the church did not wish to sanction homosexual relationships.[12] And second, marriage was declared a sacrament by the Western church in 1215. Ultimately the Latin church chose to emphasize covenant marriage over covenant friendship.[13] When Thomas Aquinas wrote the theology of the Western church in the thirteenth century, he included marriage as the only one of the seven sacraments that was not performed by a priest. In marriage, the priest functions as a witness for Christ and the one who blesses the marriage. The sacrament takes place as the couple makes public vows of faithfulness to each other. In other words, the church was a Johnny-come-lately to the marriage business. That explains why in many parts of the world the civil and religious ceremonies are separate.

Today the only hangover of the ancient friendship liturgy that remains in Western Christendom is the "godparents" portion of the infant baptism ritual.[14] The word *godparents* comes from the word *god-siblings*. Godparents make a covenant to be "siblings of God," or a spiritual big brother or sister to the child being baptized.

Covenant Renewals

According to 1 Samuel, Jonathan and David renewed their covenant on at least two occasions. That means they committed themselves to the relationship on three separate occasions (1 Samuel 18:3; 20:15–17, 22, 42; 23:18). They continued to remind each other that they had committed to a permanent, indissoluble union. And they dramatized their commitment over and over. They kept their friendship covenant fresh.

Lovers continually reassure each other of their love and commitment. Most couples celebrate each wedding anniversary. Periodic renewal-of-vows ceremonies are also common among married folks. Why, then, should not covenant friends often talk about their love for each other and fidelity to the relationship?

Once is never enough. That is why Christians participate in the Lord's Supper again and again. Each time we eat the bread and drink from the cup, we are recommitting ourselves to being part of Jesus' New Covenant community. In the same way, we should regularly reaffirm and celebrate our vows of covenant friendship.

One great covenant friendship I know of annually celebrates the day they met. Their friendship has lasted twenty-nine years, and they often celebrate that God introduced them. These two

Christian women are a dynamic duo for the Lord. One is a professional Christian musician. One is a successful Christian author. Together they create beautiful Christian hymns and songs, and they produce Christian plays and musicals. Together they have created more than one hundred published Christian books, including everything from children's books to Bibles, many of them bestsellers. Together they have led numerous overseas mission concert tours. In truth, much of the wonderful work they have done never would have happened if they had not done it as God intended . . . together.

I realize that some of you reading these words are commitment-phobic. The idea of making a serious commitment is frightening. Commitment-phobic people prefer to keep their options open. The only way you are going to experience relational and emotional fulfillment, however, is by making a covenantal commitment to another person. Some of us do not need to get married (1 Corinthians 7:1–7, 25–26, 32–35), but all of us need at least one covenant friend.

Do you have a covenant friend? Is there the equivalent of a Saturday Club in your life? Are you part of a small group that offers one another unqualified support? Who is committed to stand beside you "come hell or high water"? When things are at their worst, who are the people who will say, "I am with you; don't be afraid"? If you do not have a covenant friend, you are truly missing one of God's greatest blessings in this life. If you do not already have a covenant friend, make it a priority to find one.

CHAPTER 4

Hurts and Healings

"Relationships are not only how we become wounded;
they are how we get healed."

Jim Jackson

We were just getting to know one another. Three of us had agreed to meet every Tuesday morning at 10 a.m., rain or shine. One morning, one of the members of the group exclaimed, "I'm not sure I want to be in this group."

I followed with the obvious question: "Why not?"

He smiled and explained, "Right now you like me, but I'm not sure if you get to know the real me that you will like me."

The other member of the triad pushed for a further explanation. "What on earth are you talking about? What do you fear revealing?"

He answered with a telling anecdote: Several years ago, I hired a new administrative assistant. A couple of weeks after her employment, she walked into my office and said, "Before I came to work here, several people warned me that you were a jerk. But

I have been here long enough to know they were wrong. You are a nice guy." Her words made me feel good. But after she had been working with me for six months, she came into my office again and said to me in an exasperated tone, "I take back what I said to you several months ago. They were right. You are a jerk!"

My new friend then brought his point home: "I am afraid that when you get to know me, you will discover I am a jerk!"

Most of the people reading these words can identify with the fear of exposure suffered by my friend. If we are to be transparent with people, they may discover our character flaws and reject us. Even worse, if they discover our weaknesses and vulnerabilities, it will give them the power to hurt us. It is safer to stay at an emotional distance and do impression management.

Most of us have been deeply hurt in relationships. The more trust we have invested in the relationship and the more profound the injury, the harder it has been to get over the pain.

As I have mentioned, I spent the early years of my life in fear that if people discovered who I was, they would judge me as inferior and inadequate. So I learned to wear masks that gave me the approval I sought. I observed the behavior of those thought to be acceptable and played their roles in the story of my life. I acted in different ways around different people. Acting out these various roles gave me multiple identities, and I was uncertain which one, if any, was the real me. However, as long as I wore the right mask and kept to the appropriate scripts, I felt safe. But when I accidentally wore the wrong mask or read from the wrong script, I felt ashamed, alone, and afraid. I thought I had plenty of friends, but all of my so-called friendships were shallow and inauthentic.

There were a few times as a young man when I tried to have close friendships, but most of those relational ventures did not end well. For example, a fraternity brother stole money from me. There were several other bitter relational experiences that brought on a chain of negative emotions—disappointment, cynicism, distrust, and fear of future duplicate experiences.

I confess that I was not always the victim. There were times when I was the perpetrator. I turned the Golden Rule on its head and did to others what had been done to me. I was not the kind of friend most people valued.

Long after becoming a Christian, I found the story of my life in an ancient account in the Bible. The story of Adam and Eve, recorded in Genesis 3, is the story of every human being. The word *Adam* means "humanity" in Hebrew. My name is Adam. Your name is Adam. This ancient account explains how we got hurt relationally and how we can be healed.

We Were Created to Be Relational

Why should we bother to have friends? Friendship can be pleasurable, but it can also be excruciatingly painful. The answer from the Genesis creation story is that we were created to be relational. God is relational, and we were created in God's image (Genesis 1:26–27). In the creation story, after humans were brought into being, the Almighty said, "It is not good for humans to be alone" (Genesis 2:18). We were designed for companionship.

Think of the rest of the created order. Compared to us most of God's creation is more socially indifferent. We humans were designed for partnership. Without a counterpart, there is a gaping hole within us—that not even God can fill!

Tom Hanks starred in a Robinson Crusoe–type movie called *Cast Away*. It told the story of a FedEx employee whose plane crashed in the Pacific Ocean. He was marooned alone on a South Sea island. His only possessions during his four-year stay were the FedEx® packages that washed up on the shore. He cut his finger one day just before opening a package containing a volleyball. The blood from his finger got on the white ball, and the markings looked suspiciously like a human face. He named it "Wilson" and started carrying on conversations with it. Wilson became his only friend. One day he realized how foolish it was to talk to a volleyball. After all, it was an inanimate object. He spiked the ball off a cliff into the surf. Suddenly he realized that he had just lost his only friend, so he quickly retrieved the ball because he didn't want to be friendless. The point of the story is that we are all programmed to be relational.

Paul Wadell wrote, "Perhaps the greatest human need is a need for intimacy. Yes, to survive physically, we need food, shelter, and clothing, but to survive spiritually and emotionally, we need intimacy."[1] It is not enough to have parents, siblings, children, and employees in our life. It is easy to feel that these people have to be with us. We need friends—people who choose to share their lives with us. Without this chosen intimacy, we are spiritually and emotionally malnourished.

There is a warning in the instructions of some of the products we buy that says, "Do not try this when you are alone." When we were born, God might well have put a warning label on us saying, "It will be dangerous for this person to do life alone." We were designed for community.

The Bible says that in the beginning, Adam and Eve "walked in the garden with God in the cool of the day" (Genesis 3:8). It also says the first humans were completely vulnerable to God and to one another. They were "naked and not ashamed" (Genesis 2:25).

I like both of those images: "Walking with God" and "naked and not ashamed." These word pictures show us that originally when God and humans communicated, nothing was hidden or held back. They were open, free, and unrestrained with one another. Neither God nor the humans felt any sense of inadequacy or shame. They could say to one another whatever was in their hearts. They were naked in every sense of the word: Physically, emotionally, spiritually, and relationally. They were unashamed in every sense of the word. These word pictures sound like some distant memory to me, like a home to which I long to return.

I remember "walking with God" and being "naked and not ashamed" with God as a young child. I didn't call it prayer. I carried on a running conversation with God—and I felt no fear or shame in doing so. It was as natural as breathing. This was the place we were intended to live—in the garden of Eden—in transparency with God and a few other people.

We have a marvelous ministry in our church with people who have mental and physical challenges. It is called the "Circle of Friends." I tell people who are going through spiritual recession that they need to go and stand at that door and listen to the members of this community pray at the end of their sessions. They talk with God the way I did as a boy—before self-consciousness, concerns about how I was perceived by others, and doubts crept in and stole my innocence from me.

Watching the Circle of Friends through the years has caused me to wonder if those of us considered "normal" are not the deficient ones. Neuroscientists say the brain has two hemispheres: The left hemisphere, where rational thinking comes from; and the right hemisphere, where intuitive functions originate. The members of our Circle of Friends have good recall of facts, but they have difficulty collating unrelated information. They have difficulty taking various facts and drawing conclusions based on compiled data. But faith, a right-brain function, is no problem for them. They do not over think it. They intuitively know it is so and believe. Perhaps those of us who have trouble "walking and talking" with God and being "naked and not ashamed" with God have right-hemisphere damage!

How We Get Damaged

The story of Adam and Eve is the account of how our intimacy with God got fractured and how we became alienated from other people. Examine the story in detail with me.

The serpent said to Adam and Eve, "I have noticed that you are not eating of the tree in the midst of the garden. I was wondering why?"

Eve, speaking for Adam replied, "God told us if we ate of the tree, we would die" (Genesis 2:16–17).

The serpent contradicted what Adam and Eve had been told: "That's a lie. God is trying to hold you back. He knows if you eat of the tree, you will become a God. From then on, you will not need God. You will be able to decide for yourself what is good and what is evil. Now which would you rather be, a God or someone who has a God?"

The couple looked more carefully at the tree. Its fruit looked delicious, and they liked the idea of being a God. So they ate of the fruit of the tree. And suddenly they realized they were naked, and they sewed fig leaves together to cover their nakedness (Genesis 3:1–7).

The story of Adam and Eve is my story. And it is your story. Every one of us has done what Adam and Eve did. At some point in our lives, we have made a decision to be our own God—to decide for ourselves what is right or wrong, good or evil, rather than to have this dictated to us. Paul says, "All have sinned and fallen short of the glory of God" (Romans 3:23).

Have you ever wondered why humans wear clothes? No other members of the animal kingdom bother to do so. It has nothing to do with Madison Avenue. The most primitive humans wore clothing. According to Genesis, clothes are a confession of our relational alienation—the closeness we were created to have with God and others has been damaged. Regardless of what our nudist friends insist, when we are naked in public, we are ashamed.

When the relationship between Adam and Eve got damaged, bad things began to happen. Consider the emotional consequences that befell Adam and Eve—and us.

Fear

Adam and Eve were suddenly "afraid" of God (Genesis 3:10). That was the first sign that something had shifted in the divine-human relationship. Previously they had felt safe with the Holy One.

Fear is a sign of our internal disconnectedness with God. In the Bible, fear and faith are always juxtaposed. Over and over, Jesus said, "Do not be afraid, only believe" (Mark 4:40; 5:36). To the extent that we have fear, we do not have faith. And to the extent that we have faith, we do not have fear. When faith is dislodged, fear follows closely behind.

Fear also disrupts our relationships with other people. When trust is undermined, often because of our own actions, we are no longer willing to risk trust or self-disclosure. We opt instead for relational safety and superficiality. Intimacy requires the soil of trust to grow strong.

Shame

After their sin, Adam and Eve no longer walked and talked with God. They hid from the Almighty (Genesis 3:8). Hiding is the opposite of transparency—being "naked and not ashamed."

What a funny scene! The first humans were trying to conceal themselves from God. They were hiding from God behind a bush in the garden. Yet God is omnipresent—everywhere, including in the bush! We cannot hide from God. Jonah learned we can't run far enough to escape God's presence. The psalmist proclaimed this truth: "If I ascend to heaven, you are there. If I make my bed in hell, you are there" (Psalm 139:8).

Why were they hiding from God? Because they had done what God had told them not to do. They had eaten of the tree of knowledge of good and evil, which was the only thing God had commanded them not to do. So rather than God's presence being something they moved toward, it caused them to retreat in shame. They felt unlovable, unredeemable, and unforgivable.

When we willfully do what God tells us not to do, shame causes us to hide from God. Rather than running to God for forgiveness and grace, we withdraw from God. Instead of seeking God's mercy, we project onto God the anger we feel at ourselves. We picture God as being angry, punitive, and vengeful rather than "merciful and gracious, slow to anger, and abounding in steadfast love" (Nehemiah 9:17; Psalm 103:8; 145:8; Joel 2:13; Jonah 4:2).

Do you know why some people who say they believe in God's grace so rarely confess their sins to God? Because they do not want the Almighty to find out what they have been doing or not doing. These people lightly say, "Lord, forgive me for all my sins." But this isn't a true confession; it is a detour around confession.

In addition to causing us to withdraw from our relationship with God, internalized shame causes us to withdraw from our relationships with other people—to isolate ourselves, to hide. Shame focuses us on self-protection rather than intimacy. Our instinct is to hide the truth about ourselves so we will not be discovered or humiliated. Sometimes we even sabotage relationships to protect people from the harm they could experience by knowing us.

Blame

Adam blamed the whole mess on Eve. Blaming Eve diminished his feeling of guilt and brought him some sense of comfort. Blaming is about self-defense.

In another way, he actually blamed God. Adam said, "The woman you gave to be with me. . ." (Genesis 3:13). Now and then, I hear a couple in love say that God picked out their mate for them. Usually I remain quiet, but what I want to say is, "God hasn't picked out a mate for anyone since Adam blamed God for having given him Eve!"

Eve said she wasn't responsible, either. She blamed everything on the serpent (Genesis 3:13). The shifting of blame away from ourselves to someone else is toxic to relationships. Pointing the finger of blame always injures the relationship.

Blaming is also dishonest. It blinds us from seeing our part in the drama. For example, listen to the words of the story: "When the woman saw that the fruit of the tree was good for food and pleasing to the eye, and also desirable for gaining wisdom, she took some and ate it. She also gave some to her husband, who was with her, and he ate it" (Genesis 3:6). Adam participated fully in Eve's decision by passively going along with what she was doing. He was complicit in every way.

When we blame others for what happened, we tell a partial lie in order to feel better about ourselves. It is a way of treating the relationship as expendable.

Wearing Masks

Adam and Eve "sewed fig leaves together and made loin-clothes for themselves" to cover their nakedness (Genesis 3:7). What do fig leaves represent? They are the masks we wear to conceal our vulnerability. They are false identities, pretend selves. Fig leaves are designed to keep the inadequate, imperfect, and immature parts of ourselves from being exposed. We want people to see our fig leaves instead of the naked truths about ourselves. William Shakespeare put it this way: "God hath given you one face and you make yourself another."[2]

It is impossible to have an intimate relationship with a person who is wearing a mask. The whole purpose of a mask is to prevent being known. We wear masks because we want to appear to be someone we are not. The worst part about masks is that we start taking our pretend selves seriously. We confuse our fig leaves with our real selves.

Many of us wear professional masks. Someone asks us, "Who are you?" and we answer with a professional identity, such as, "I'm a teacher," or "I'm a computer tech." That is what we do, not who we are. A professional identity is a fig leaf.

Some people wear religious masks, pretending to be more devout than they actually are. Jesus often called the religious leaders of his day "hypocrites"—literally mask-wearers.

It is amazing how long and how well people can carry on a masquerade. Now and then, we hear or read about someone who was caught doing something inconsistent with his or her public persona. His or her mask was exposed as a sham. Jesus said that one day, something like this will happen to all of us. He promised, "For nothing is hidden that will not be disclosed, nor is anything secret that will not become known and come to light" (Luke 8:17; 12:2).

Denial

It is possible to exhibit one or more of the characteristics we have been discussing—fear, shame, blame, wearing masks— and have no knowledge of it. The terrible thing about denial is that we fool ourselves. When Adam denied that he had any responsibility for violating the command of God, he really believed what he was saying. Denial operates below the level of consciousness. We might be able to see these negative behaviors in others, but we honestly do not see them in ourselves.

I have attended many addiction interventions through the years. In these gatherings, alcohol and/or drug abusers are lovingly confronted by family members and friends and asked to go to a treatment facility for help. Unfortunately, most of these interventions have been unsuccessful. The people being confronted were convinced they did not have a problem. They were sure that they could quit drinking or drugging any time they wanted. They just didn't want to—at least not at that time. That is called "denial." Denial rationalizes, justifies, and calls maladaptive behavior normal.

We are probably in denial when someone points out our behavior and we react in one of the following two ways:

1. Anger. We get touchy. When someone points out our fear, shaming, blaming, or masking, we become defensive. We justify what we are doing. If necessary, we go on the offensive against them, pointing out their flaws. We will do whatever is necessary to push them away. I remember doing something like that with my own wife and children: "Of course I'm not a workaholic!" I exclaimed. "Someone has to provide for this family!" Solomon said, "If someone wants to know the truth, they are willing to be set right, but anyone who hates to be admonished is a stupid idiot" (Proverbs 12:1).

2. Self-sufficiency. We say to ourselves, "I can change if I try harder." We fail to see that we are enslaved, even addicted. What sounds like confidence on the surface is actually overconfidence, and it guarantees that the destructive behavior will continue—and get worse. We need the power of God and the support of other people to break the negative behavioral patterns.

Lest we think all is lost because we identify with the struggles of Adam and Eve, permit me to offer a radical insight: Failure to live up to all we believe in is what enables us to grow to a higher level of spiritual transformation. When we fail to measure up to the behavioral standards of our faith, we are forced to shift the basis of our faith from law (keeping the rules perfectly) to gospel (complete trust in God's undeserved and unrepayable grace), from external governance (living up to the rules of our religious institutions) to internal governance (depending solely on the Holy Spirit), from spiritual overconfidence (thinking we can keep all the rules) to profound humility (the realization that we cannot keep all the rules).

How We Get Healed

How do we recover our lost innocence? How can we "walk with God" and become "naked and not ashamed" once more? The answer, as stated earlier, is God's grace. God never gives us what we deserve. He gives us what we need. The psalmist sang, "If you, O Lord, should keep a record of wrongs, who could stand? But there is forgiveness with you. . ." (130:3–4).

One of my favorite gospel stories is the account of Jesus raising Lazarus from the dead (John 11:38–44). The stone that had covered the tomb for three days was rolled away, and the resuscitated man came out hopping. He was hopping because his body was bound by grave wrappings. The stench of his previously decaying flesh was still on him. Jesus said to those gathered around, "Unbind him and set him free." Like Lazarus, it is not enough for us to be raised to new life—to become new creations. We need to be unbound—set free from the stench of our former life. But we cannot unbind ourselves. The redemptive work of healing the damage done by fear, shaming, blaming, masking, and denial requires community. We cannot heal ourselves.

God's gracious desire to restore us to our previous relationship is demonstrated in the Genesis account (Genesis 3:8–24). Notice five important expressions of God's grace as seen in Genesis.

Friends Take the Initiative

God seized the initiative in his relationship to Adam and Eve. God did not wait for them to come to him. Instead, he sought them out.

Notice the way in which the Almighty came to Adam and Eve. God did not quickly or impulsively intervene in Adam and Eve's life. He did not confront them bluntly or in anger. He entered the garden and gently called out to them, saying, "Where are you?" (Genesis 3:9).

Had God lost Adam and Eve? Of course not. He knew exactly where they were. If I had been God, I probably would have brusquely confronted them, saying, "Do you think I am blind? I see you there, behind the bush! I see the fig leaves you are wearing! Come out here immediately and face the music!" But God was not invasive or offensive. He wanted Adam and Eve to come out of hiding on their own.

Friends are willing to take the initiative in relationships, but they do not intrude. They call out to us and then wait for us to feel safe enough to join them.

When a friendship gets bruised, we do our best to maintain contact with them. We write to them, call to check on them, do good things for them, say nice things about them, and pray for them (Matthew 5:38–48).

Friends Ask Hard Questions

When Adam and Eve came out of hiding, God asked them hard questions: "Where are you? Who told you that you were naked? Have you eaten from the tree of which I commanded you not to eat?" (Genesis 3:9, 11). Did God not know the answers to these questions? Of course he knew. He asked these questions not to get an answer, but to confront Adam and Eve with the truth of the situation they had created.

Friends ask penetrating questions. We all need someone who cares about us enough to ask us hard questions—the kinds of questions that pierce our walls of denial.

I will never forget meeting with a friend many years ago. I was complaining about a staff member I was having trouble motivating to do his job. My friend put the right question to me gently but firmly: "Tell me, Jim. Why do you put up with that?"

I answered, "I'm not sure."

His question clarified what I needed to do. I went back to the office and fired the employee.

Learning how to ask the right question in the right way is a critically important relational skill both in professional relationships and in friendships. We need to think before we speak, frame our questions in noncritical ways, and "speak the truth in love" (Ephesians 4:15). Don't expect an answer. Ask the question and add, "Just think about it."

Friends Tell Us the Truth

God told Adam and Eve the truth. Now it was time for "reality therapy." God told them the consequences of their behavior (Genesis 3:14–19). He was not criticizing them. The Almighty was being honest with them.

We all need people in our lives who do not parrot conventional wisdom or merely tell us what we want to hear. We need authentic friends who will tell us the truth, even if it is unpleasant. Solomon said, "Whoever rebukes a person will afterward find more favor than one who flatters with the tongue" (Proverbs 28:23).

I was with a cousin I love dearly not long ago. We had not seen each other in a long time. While we were together, she made a comment about my weight. She was not criticizing me. She was expressing loving concern for my health. Rather than resenting her comment, I appreciated it. Her candor helped me resolve to lose some weight.

Paul advises us to "speak the truth in love" (Ephesians 4:15). Truth without tenderness is a bludgeon. A Chinese proverb puts it this way: "Do not remove a fly from your friend's head with a hatchet."[3]

Friends Hang in There with Us

God did not give up on Adam and Eve. He hung in there with them. God told Adam and Eve that if they ate of the tree of knowledge of good and evil, they would die (Genesis 2:17). But they did not die! Some argue that they died spiritually (1 Corinthians 15:22), and others suggest that prior to their sin, Adam and Eve were created to live a physical life eternally. Maybe so, but they certainly did not immediately die physically—which appears to be what God promised. Their lives, physically and spiritually, were preserved by God's grace. Adam lived many more years—930 years in all (Genesis 5:5). Second Peter 3:9 says, "God is patient with you, not wanting any to perish, but all to come to repentance."

At the conclusion of each worship service at the church where I served, the Aaronic Blessing is pronounced—the one God gave to Aaron, Moses' brother and Israel's first priest. Aaron was told to use these words to bless God's people (Numbers 6:24–26). The blessing begins, "The Lord bless you and keep you." Here is my translation of this phrase: "Because you have sinned, you do not deserve to continue to live. But may the Lord keep you around anyway. May you not get what you deserve."

The most concrete expression of God's grace is Jesus of Nazareth. Paul calls him "the second Adam"—the second representative of humanity (Romans 5:12–21; 1 Corinthians 15:45–49). Jesus' preferred name for himself was "Son of Man"—or "Son of the Human Being (Adam)." Paul argued that the first Adam was the representative of all humanity. Adam represented us perfectly because we have all made the same decision he made—we have chosen to be our own God and to decide for ourselves what is good or evil (Genesis 3:1–5). He further proclaims that those who identify with Jesus are restored to a pre-sin Adam and Eve relationship with God. We "walk and talk with God"; we are "naked and not ashamed."

There are some pretty tough laws in the Bible. For example, the Jewish law commanded that stubborn and rebellious children be stoned (Deuteronomy 21:18–21). How many of us would have survived to adulthood? But Bible scholars tell us that the most severe laws like this one were never practiced. People were given better than they deserved.

Friends also give their friends better than they deserve. Friends do not throw us away when they discover the worst about us. They give us the same grace God gave them (Ephesians 4:32). Regardless of what we do, friends continue to see us from a spiritual rather than a human perspective (2 Corinthians 5:16). They see in us not just what we are but what we can become.

Friends Respect Our Boundaries

God respected Adam and Eve's boundaries. The account ends with a remarkable verse: "And the Lord God made garments of skin for the man and his wife, and clothed them" (Genesis 3:21). God became the first tailor, swapping their temporary fig leaves for permanent animal skins. God was telling them, and us, that it is unsafe to walk around in our world emotionally exposed. It is unwise to be relationally vulnerable with everyone we meet. There are some people with whom it is not wise to share our innermost thoughts. And there are people with whom we do not need to enter a covenant relationship.

What Genesis calls "clothes" would be labeled "boundaries" in contemporary parlance. In other words, the need for boundaries is as old as Adam and Eve. Each of us has to set emotional limits in order to create a zone of safety for ourselves. Boundaries say to other persons, "You are responsible for those things, and I am responsible for these things." In his poem "The Mending Wall," Robert Frost wrote, "Good fences make good neighbors."[4] He was right. There are all sorts of boundary lines—

verbal, physical, sexual, moral, financial, and relational. We need to know what our boundaries are and how we are going to maintain them.

Solomon advised, "Guard your heart, for out of it flow the springs of life" (Proverbs 4:23). Biblically the heart is not the muscle in our chest. It is who we are on the inside. In other words, protect who you are, because everything you do and say comes out of your heart. Jesus taught the exact same principle (Luke 6:45).

One way to think about boundaries is as a moat that separates land from a castle. If we are the castle and the moat is our boundary, then the drawbridge is the means by which we invite people into relationships. Letting down one's drawbridge should be done on a discriminating basis. It is a mistake to live with one's drawbridge down.

Boundaries are the breathing spaces we need between ourselves and others. There are people with whom we need a great deal of distance and others with whom we can be much more intimate, but we need boundaries in all our relationships. Kahlil Gibran said, "Let there be spaces in your togetherness."[5]

Sexual intimacy occurs when we pull back our boundaries and become "naked and not ashamed" with someone (Genesis 2:25). It is a slice of heaven in which we will be universally exposed to all of redeemed humanity.

Notice that the father of the prodigal son in Jesus' famous parable (Luke 15:11–24) not only let his son go, but refused to rescue him. The father, who represents God, did not go to the far country and coax his son to come home. He did not smuggle care packages to the far country to keep his son from eating hog slop. The father let his precious son, who represents us, enjoy a banquet of consequences (Luke 15:11–16). And when the prodigal son returned home and wanted to assume the role of a servant, the father did not allow him to become a dependent person (Luke 15:18–24). God is a respecter of boundaries.

People without boundaries are dangerous to themselves and others. Only when we have boundaries are we truly self-respecting and respectful of others. Proverbs 25:28 says, "Like a city whose walls have been breached and destroyed is one who lacks boundaries." We have a right to say no to people, to not fulfill their expectations, to decide who our friends will be. We have a right to healthy boundaries.

Here is why we need to set healthy boundaries early in a friendship:

- so friends will not have unrealistic expectations of us
- so friends will not intrude in our personal, relational, or professional life in ways that will lead to resentment
- so friends will not rely on us for their sole support, which will lead to burn-out and codependency
- so friends will not feel rejected later when we draw boundaries

It is a good idea to go slow in new friendships, to put a governor on the pace at which we make ourselves vulnerable. We should let people prove themselves to be trustworthy before we give them weapons that can be used against us.

Most of us struggle with what Ralph Earle and Susan Metsner call the "intimacy paradox."[6] One voice within us says, "Do you see those people over there? Tell them to come closer to you." The other voice says, "No, tell them to go away. Don't let them get too close to you." These two forces pull on us like centrifugal and centripetal forces in the universe—one drawing us in, the other pulling us away—one urging us to be known, the other telling us to pull away and hide our weaknesses. Which voice will we choose to listen to? I, for one, have decided to lean in the direction of being known. I do not want to be unwise or indiscriminate about friendships. But I would rather risk the fragility of life as a butterfly than remain in a safe emotional cocoon.

Why have friends? Because relationships not only are how we become wounded; they are how we get healed. As our intimacy with God increases, so should our intimacy with others. Likewise, as human relationships deepen, so should our friendship with God. The two relationships should grow together in harmony.

By the way, the fellow who feared he might be exposed as a jerk is still my friend. We no longer meet on Tuesday mornings because we no longer live in the same city, but we have maintained a covenant relationship through the years. We have each taken initiative, asked hard questions, told the truth, persevered, and respected boundaries. That is what friends do for each other.

CHAPTER 5

How to Choose Friends Wisely

*"Be courteous to all, but intimate with few,
and let those few be well tried before you give them your
confidence."*

George Washington

The old English proverb is correct: "A friend of all is a friend of none." And since choosing our friends is one of the most important decisions we make in life, we must choose wisely.

Isn't it interesting what great lengths we go to in order to find the right physician, dentist, lawyer, CPA, counselor? We search the Internet and ask people for recommendations. Sometimes we even interview potential professional, before using them. But when it comes to searching for friends, the people we will walk beside in life, we take a haphazard approach. Or we fish in shallow water, looking for relationships in the wrong places. How much sense does that make? Beyond our family members, whom we do not choose, no one determines the outcome of our lives more than our friends. Friends are the difference between black-and-white living and high-definition living.

Solomon made a wise observation: "Whoever walks with the wise becomes wise, but the companion of fools suffers harm" (Proverbs 13:20). To walk with someone is to choose to live life with him, to be his permanent companion. This proverb assumes that the values of the people we are closest to eventually seep into our lives. If we walk with people who are wise, their wisdom will become part of us. If we walk with people who have difficulty finding true north on their moral compasses, we will eventually do foolish things ourselves. The closer we are to people, the more influence they have in our lives and the more like them we become. It is not just teenagers who experience peer pressure! We are all influenced by others, no matter our age.

That does not mean we should snub the people we consider morally repugnant. No! We are to love them, be kind to them, and serve them. We just don't draft them as members of our relational team.

Some people claim to be unaffected by their relationships. I have heard people say, "I am who I am. No one influences me." But they are wrong. Everyone in our social network affects us. We are emotionally hardwired to mirror the people around us. Knowingly and unknowingly, positively and negatively, other people influence us. We find ourselves mimicking their words and actions. It is contagious—no exceptions!

People in recovery from addictive disorders have to find alternative peer groups, usually some sort of Twelve Step program. If they remain tightly connected to their old peer groups, their risk of relapse is high. Similarly, people who have spiritual transformations need a new set of friends. Why? Because our peer groups have a big influence on our behavior.

Not all influences are negative. We have good people around us who make it easier to do the right thing. In other words, those of us who are morally upright are not so entirely because we are pure by nature. Some of the credit belongs to those who set good examples for us.

Our friends bring out the best and the worst in us. Without friends, whole sides of our nature would be unknown and unexpressed.

It doesn't sound very religious, but I have come to believe that our relationships have more power over our behavior than does our belief system. Simon Peter protested that he would never betray Jesus, but when he had hung out in the courtyard of the high priest for a while, he denied Jesus—not once but three times (Mark 14:29–31, 66–72). I don't care how strong our convictions are; if we hang around with the wrong people long enough, we eventually will do things we think we are incapable of doing. Paul wrote, "Bad company ruins good morals" (1 Corinthians 15:33).

Some will ask, "What about Jesus? Wasn't he 'a friend of tax collectors and sinners'"? (Matthew 11:19). Yes, absolutely. But Jesus was influencing them; they were not influencing him. Few of us are as morally fixed as Jesus. In most situations, those who are the least moral exercise the most influence. Furthermore, tax collectors and sinners were not invited into Jesus' inner circle until they repented and made God's kingdom and righteous living their first priority (Matthew 6:33).

What to Look for in a Friend

Proverbs 12:26 counsels, "The righteous choose their friends carefully." Along the way, I have told many people who made one poor choice after another, "Your 'picker' is broken." Scripture has a lot to say about what to look for in a friend. Following these insights might fix our pickers. We need all the help we can get to narrow the field of candidates for our friendship team.

Ethical People

First, choose friends who are highly ethical. Aelred of Rievaulx observed, "Friendship cannot exist among the wicked."[1] If you discover a lack of honesty or faulty character in a potential friend, exclude him or her. We can work with them, play with them, love them, serve them, and witness to them, but we should not invite them into our inner circle.

Proverbs 6:16-19 gives us seven integrity red flags to look for:

1.   Haughty eyes. Solomon warned about people who carry themselves with an air of arrogance. They expect to be treated with deference. They lack humility. Their eyes say, "I matter, and you don't." My experience with arrogant people is that their seeming superiority is a cover for insecurity or shame.

2.   A lying tongue. Since we cannot know what is going on in the heart of another person, friendship must be based on trust. Liars are untrustworthy and dangerous.

3.   Hands that shed innocent blood. Solomon had people other than murderers in mind. He included people with anger issues, people who lack compassion, people who feel no pangs of conscience when the weak are victimized and the innocent are dealt with unjustly, and people who disclose confidences.

4.   A heart that devises wicked plans. Steer clear of people who are good at developing plans that are shady, deceptive, or borderline illegal. These people can rationalize anything. We have all known innocent people who have gotten into legal trouble because of their association with disreputable people.

5.   Feet that hurriedly run to evil. Beware of people who are impulsive, who have more enthusiasm than good sense. They get caught up in ill-fated, get-rich-quick schemes. And they will pull us into the ditch with them.

6.   A lying witness who testifies falsely. Some people will lie to anyone, including when they are under oath. Beware of people

who are dishonest—who have a lack of respect for authority, promises, oaths, and the rule of law.

7. One who sows discord in a family. These people enjoy stirring the pot of conflict at home. They often disrespect marriage vows. They consider strife to be normal. Notice the result of this person's presence: Do they leave chaos or peace in their wake?

We all know people with one or more of these seven characteristics. Stay away from them! Do not choose to partner with them. It is not necessarily true that "a friend in need is a friend indeed." "A friend in need" with the wrong values is a pest! And, no, our love will not change them. Their negative qualities are more likely to seep into our lives.

What, then, are the qualities of integrity that we should seek in a friend? Flip Solomon's negative characteristics on their head, look for the polar opposite qualities, and you will find the answer. We need friends who are. . .

- humble
- truthful
- compassionate
- moral
- cautious
- law abiders
- peacemakers

General Stonewall Jackson advised, "Seek friends who are intelligent and virtuous, and if possible, those who are a little above you, especially in moral excellence."[2]

Positive People

Second, choose friends whose nature it is to be positive. We need friends who will put something into us, not take something from us. We all know people who deplete us. Negative people are forever criticizing, complaining, and condemning. They spread gloom and doom everywhere they go. They are life-suckers. We need life-givers.

Terrible things happened to Job. He lost his family, his wealth, and his health. Yet Job was able to endure all this—until his three negative friends showed up. It was their pessimistic words and spirit that finally broke him. To their credit, they did at least show up. Even better, they grieved with him in silence for seven days. They sat there, like psychotherapists, waiting for Job to break the silence. But when they started talking, they would not shut up! They talked for twenty-eight chapters, from chapter 3 through chapter 31! They served Job "prepackaged truth in just-add-water containers."[3] They offered a string of unsolicited clichés and advice. They played the role of God instead of friend. Nothing makes us feel more lonely than having to endure the presence of people who do not understand us but continuously offer us advice we cannot use. Here is a summary of what Job's three friends said to him:

Eliphaz said, "The reason you are having all these problems is that you are a big sinner! If you accept God's discipline and repent, God will restore your peace and prosperity" (Job 4:8, 17; 5:17–27).

Bildad said, "Your problem is you were an indulgent father. You are being punished for your children's sins. If you cleanse yourself and pray hard, God will restore you to your rightful place" (Job 8:4–6).

Zophar said, "You need to straighten out your theology. It's simple: Bad people have problems, and good people prosper. Evidently you have committed a heinous sin. Repent, and everything will be all right again" (Job 11:5–6, 14, 20).

With friends like those, who needs enemies? In response, Job accused them of withholding kindness from him (Job 6:14; 19:21). But in spite of their lack of support, Job managed to pray for his friends (Job 42:10). Most of us could not have survived the kind of negative onslaught that came his way. I have trouble being around negative people for very long.

Since our friends have an effect on us, doesn't it make sense that we would choose friends who think and act positively?

Emotionally Healthy People

A third characteristic to look for in a friend is good mental health. Several years ago, I heard psychologist Les Parrott say, "Your relationships can only be as healthy as the least healthy person in them." Paul D. O'Callaghan said a similar thing: "True friendship requires people who are sufficiently whole so as not to be driven by major character deficiencies."[4]

Proverbs 22:24–25 gives us a specific example of the kind of emotionally toxic people we should avoid: "Make no friends with those given to anger, and do not associate with hotheads, or you may learn their ways and entangle yourself in a snare." Anger is highly contagious.

There are people who are unsafe. They are so psychologically injured that they injure other people. The Twelve Step community says this somewhat differently: "Hurt people—hurt people." We should never offer our hearts to people who destroy hearts.

One of the most insightful poems ever written is Martin Buber's "I and Thou." It talks about two different kinds of relationships: "I-It" and "I-Thou" relationships. We are in an I-It relationship when we view the other person as an object. I-It relationships are narcissistic. In them, we see the world revolving around us. When we look at I-It people, we want to know if they are going to hurt us or help us. We use I-It people to make our lives better. I-It friendships are about mutual exploitation and barter. Some people even see God as an "It." They see God not as Father, but as a resource from which we extract what we want to enhance our lives. Prayer, therefore, is a monologue through which we give God a grocery list of our needs and wants. If we do not get what we have asked for, we get angry with God. People who offer an I-It relationship make poor covenant friends.

Buber says we are in an "I-Thou" relationship when we see the other person as a creature of sacred worth. People are "Thous" when we treat them with honor, dignity, and respect. We are interested in I-Thou people for who they are, not for what they can do for us. God is the ultimate "Thou," and we are interested in God for God's sake. And prayer is a dialogue between friends. People who are capable of I-Thou relationships make good covenant friends. We need friends who can offer us healthy companionship.

Characteristics of Worthwhile Friends

1. They have a positive concept of themselves, and they encourage others to have a positive self-concept.
2. They have a sense of humor, including having a belly laugh every now and then.
3. They have a unifying and well-thought-out philosophy of life that defines their understanding of reality.
4. They find enjoyment in helping other people, but they do so without losing themselves.
5. They live in the present tense, rather than in the past (guilt) or the future (anxiety).
6. They have a hopeful view of the future.
7. They accept full responsibility for the shape their lives have taken; they do not blame their problems on other people or expect others to take care of them.
8. They have a conscious awareness of their feelings and then manage them.
9. They are able to practice self-discipline and self-restraint; they can say no to themselves.

10. They are accepting and respectful of people from different ethnic and racial backgrounds, people who hold different views, and people who make different choices. They realize that somehow they are connected to every other human being.
11. They are able to differentiate between the things they can change and the things they cannot change. They attempt to change the things they can change and they leave alone the things they cannot change.
12. They do what needs to be done, when it needs to be done, whether they feel like doing it or not.
13. They practice deferred gratification.
14. They love people and use things, rather than loving things and using people.
15. They know their weaknesses and limitations, and they are vigilant about them.
16. They are able to exercise discretion, hold confidences, and keep commitments.
17. They forgive themselves and others, even though the wrong is still remembered.
18. They are able to learn from past mistakes rather than repeating them; they are also able to learn from the mistakes of others rather than learning everything the hard way.
19. They are capable of transparency, vulnerability, and self-disclosure when it is appropriate, but they are not emotional exhibitionists.
20. They have boundaries, and they respect the boundaries of other people.
21. They are assertive enough to ask for what they need, and they are kind and gentle in doing it.
22. They do not fear change; they see it as an opportunity to grow and to make things the way they could have been all along.
23. They see their mission in life as being aimed at the intersection of the world's need and their unique gift mix.

24. They are dedicated to living in integrity; they refuse to speak or practice untruth and deception.
25. They are never afraid of the truth.
26. They do not have an opinion on every subject.
27. They realize that there may not be a solution to every problem.
28. They live in faith that there will always be enough for them, and so they are able to be generous to others.
29. They do not have an excessive need for recognition or impression management; they are more concerned with truth than with what others think.
30. They respond with compassion to the needs they can meet; they are responsive to the simple cry of human need.
31. They live in harmony with their body, they are not self-indulgent, and they handle their sexuality appropriately.
32. They are teachable; they are always eager to learn, especially from the people around them.
33. They are not perfectionists; they carry flexible expectations and still find contentment in themselves.
34. They do not seek to control other people, and they offer few opinions. They let people learn their own lessons.
35. They are not unduly attached to or detached from their family of origin.
36. They are not controlled by addictive disorders and do not seek to control others through codependency.
37. They are capable of unconditional love.
38. They are sensitive, intuitive, and discerning of the people around them.
39. They make good ethical decisions; they consistently do the next right thing.
40. They find something good in the people they meet and in the experiences they have.
41. They are able to suffer loss and pain without blaming other people or God.

42. They strive for relational unity, harmony, cooperation, reconciliation, and peace.
43. They are able to run reasonable risks without excessive fear.
44. They have interdependent, mutually fulfilling relationships with friends.
45. They do not wear masks or maintain false selves; they are the same person regardless of who they are around.
46. They have the will to remain faithful to worthy purposes, regardless of the outcome or personal costs.
47. They notice nature; they are inquisitive of the world around them.
48. They are genuinely spiritual, and their spirituality produces the fruits of God's Spirit within them—love, joy, peace, patience, kindness, goodness, gentleness, faithfulness, and self- control.
49. They have made their peace that when life is over, the things to which they have given themselves will remain unfinished, and that much of what they have learned cannot be passed along to others.
50. They realize that they are emotionally broken, they are aware of their areas of brokenness, and they are committed to healing these wounds.

Jesus had all of these qualities, except number 50. None of us has all fifty of these qualities. Part of what it means to be human is that the image of God is defaced in us (Genesis 1:26–27; Romans 3:23). We all have flaws and deficiencies, which is all the more reason it is imperative that our friends exhibit character quality number 50. Beyond this, choose friends with as many of these fifty qualities as possible. It is all right to have a friend or two who is an emotional struggler. After all, we hope someone will pick us.

Spiritually Integrated People

Fourth, choose friends who are genuinely spiritual. The Apocrypha says, "Associate with a godly person whom you know to be keeping the commandments, who is like-minded with yourself, and who will grieve with you if you fail" (Sirach 37:12). We need friends who consider a relationship with God to be of primary interest and concern.

Friendships among spiritual equals involves more than face-to-face conversation. It includes intercessory prayer. When both parties have a spiritual perspective on life (Galatians 6:1), it is as natural as breathing to bring one another into the presence of God.

Should all our friends be Christians? Many Christians answer with an emphatic "Yes!" They quote the apostle Paul to bolster their case: "Do not be mismatched with unbelievers" (2 Corinthians 6:14). This verse calls to mind the image of oxen connected by means of a wooden yoke, a picture of partnership. But does this passage negate the possibility of friendships with people from other religious backgrounds or with no religious convictions? I appeal to the authority of Jesus in this matter: "Whoever is not against us is for us" (Mark 9:40).

Most of my close friends are Christians. Our faith is part of our bond. But I have other friends I think of as "pre-Christian." We are friends because I have a strong sense of call to the relationship. I wish they were Christians. I speak plainly to them about the difference faith makes in my life. I pray for them every day. At times, our faith differences have put a strain on the friendship. However, our friendship is not contingent on their professing faith in Jesus or going to church. That would make the friendship manipulative.

I like what Augustine said about friendship in a sermon: "He truly loves a friend who loves God in the friend, either because God is actually present in the friend or in order that God might be so present."[5] In other words, whether or not a person is a believer, God is still at work in the relationship as long as it is not born of a desire for some carnal or temporal advantage.

I would not counsel you to exclude all non-Christians from your list of potential friends. However, unbelievers should not be your closest friends, and friendship with unbelievers should be an exception rather than the rule.

How to Search for a Friend

Now that we know what we are looking for in a friend, how do we go about searching for one?

Pray

First, we should ask God to help us in the search. One of God's names in the Old Testament is Jehovah Jireh—literally, "the Lord our Provider." Why would we not ask our Provider for assistance in such an important matter? Doesn't the Bible teach that "every good and perfect gift" comes from God? (James 1:17). Paul asked, "What do you have that you did not receive?" (1 Corinthians 4:7). And Jesus taught us to pray for "daily bread" (Matthew 6:11)—for God to give us what we need to be adequately nourished as persons. What do we need more than friendship? Through prayer, we invite God into this equation.

Prayer is also a means of discerning whether we should add people to our friendship team. Just because a person happens into our life after we have prayed, this doesn't mean that it is God's will for us to invite them to be a covenant friend. We need to ask God to help us discern whether the person meets our criteria.

Look

Second, we need to be on the lookout for friends. The suffix "-ship" in friendship implies that we are to be actively involved in the search for friends.[6]

When our sons went to college, I offered them a single piece of advice: "Spend the next four years looking for four friends you will keep up with from now on." I warned them that there would be many relational false starts and unhappy endings, but that the search itself would give them relational skills that would be useful for the rest of their lives. I have since discovered that the same message should be given to people at every stage of life—whether they are entering elementary school or the nursing home.

There are an unlimited number of places to look for friends. Church and ministry activities are an obvious place to start. We are more likely to find people with the above five qualities within the community of faith than in a bar. But we do not have to limit our search to church activities. Why not use the same networking strategies we would use in searching for a job or prospecting for new clients? Be creative. Look for new ways to connect with people. Use social network opportunities, such as Facebook, Twitter®, My Space®, and LinkedIn. Participate in existing organizations, clubs, and groups. Take advantage of Starbucks® bulletin boards, and even free publicity in community newspapers to find like-minded potential friends.

Invite

Third, develop a prospective friendship list. Add people to the list who have the qualities you are looking for. Take the initiative. Jesus told his apostles, "You did not choose me, but I chose you" (John 15:16). Start inviting these people to participate in coffees, dinners, recreational outings, and social events. Offer hospitality.

If you do not know the people you would like to invite, ask someone who knows them for an introduction.

It all goes back to the old law of "sowing and reaping" (Galatians 6:7–9). Elbert Hubbard wrote, "If you would have a friend, be one."[7] Be the kind of friend to them that you would like someone to be for you, which includes these traits:

- being a good listener
- being thoughtful and complimentary
- being appreciative
- avoiding arguments and conflict
- keeping confidences
- practicing the Golden Rule (Matthew 7:12)

Cultivate and Test

Fourth, start to plow deeper. Ask probing questions—the kind of questions whose answers reveal a person's worldview, beliefs, behaviors, and philosophy of life. In theology, we call what we are looking for a "hermeneutical principle," or a principle of interpretation. Assuming that people are honest, once you know their core selves, you know them. And you can accurately predict how they will respond to any question or in any situation.

Over time, move the discussions from the shallow end to the deep end of the pool. Risk some self-disclosure:

- express some vulnerabilities
- admit some mistakes
- discuss your position on some controversial issues
- come clean about some of your questions and doubts

Test the relationship. Trust them with more and more of your heart. Jesus said, "Whoever is faithful in a very little is faithful also in much; and whoever is dishonest in a very little is dishonest also in much" (Luke 16:10). Some folks will drop out as the relationship starts into deeper water. All they want is a shallow friendship. That's fine. But make a decision that shallow friendships are not what you want in your inner circle.

I have had many friendship false starts along the way. For some reason, the relationship either stopped growing, or one of us decided it was not worth further development. Either way, the relationship remained friendly but did not become a covenant friendship.

Let me warn those of you who are wealthy, powerful, influential, or famous that choosing friends is much more difficult for you than for others. You must test potential friends with much more care than does the ordinary person. There are two reasons for this disadvantage. First, you are likely to be a highly competitive person—and competition kills relationships! The thing that helped you achieve worldly success is a relational disadvantage to you. And second, many people will want to be close to you in order to extract some benefit. Test friends carefully before bonding to them. Proverbs 20:5 counsels, "The purposes in the human mind are like deep water, but a discerning person will draw them out."

Patience

Finally, don't be in a hurry. Paul says, "Test everything; hold fast to that which is good" (1 Thessalonians 5:21). Nothing worthwhile grows quickly. It is not likely that when you first meet a person, you are going to be close friends, but a spark of interest may be ignited. It is likely that you will have many false starts. But even when friendships work from the beginning, it takes time for trust to build.

Spend time together. Tell the story of your life to one another. Confide in one another. Build a common history. Give the friendship time to grow organically, without pressure or obligation.

A wise friend once said, "You never really know a person until you have seen them in a crunch." Watch the way your potential friends negotiate the tough times. What people do when things are at their worst and their backs are against the wall says a lot about them.

Remember that nothing in life stays fixed, including friendships. Take time to do the continual care and maintenance that friendship requires.

Analogy: A Garden

Learn to think of your friends as a garden. Expert gardeners advise that if you want to grow a luscious year-round garden, you have to grow a variety of plants and keep them in different stages of development. The same could be said of friends. We need a variety of friends, and we need them at different stages of development. Our friendships need to be budding, growing, developing, and changing continually. Friendships are dynamic. Some of today's casual relationships might well become tomorrow's intimate friends.

Hugh Prather writes about the stages newly forming friendships go through: At first we see each other's virtues, then we see each other's faults, and finally we can see each other, and we become friends.[8]

New Acquaintances

We need to be continually meeting new people. Logan Pearsall Smith wrote, "We need new friends; some of us are cannibals who have eaten their old friends up."[9] Unfortunately, that is an accurate statement for many people.

New acquaintances are exciting. It is fun to get to know new people and see the relationship grow. Start slow with new relationships. Don't risk too much, too soon. Do not be an emotional exhibitionist. Do what the turtle does: Stick your neck out and see if it is safe to proceed. If the risk feels too great, pull back. The Apocrypha advises, "When you gain friends, gain them through testing, and do not trust them hastily" (Sirach 6:7).

Developing Friendships

Realize that not all friendships continue to develop. It is good that some of them fade, because none of us has the time necessary to maintain an abundance of close friendships.

Each of us has a limited number of connecting points. Leif Anderson has observed that people are more like LEGO® building blocks than Velcro®. Velcro can be attached in an unlimited number of places, but LEGO building blocks have only one to eight snap points. Like LEGO, each of us has a different relational capacity. Sometimes we can't have the right kind of friends because we are "coupled up" with the wrong people. We have to unplug from our existing friendships in order to have optimal friendships. Other times we are not able to have the friendships we need because other people are coupled up. The best we can do is to be on their "waiting list."[10]

It is important to invest in the development of new friendships. When I was a boy, I noticed that many of my elderly grandmother's best friends were younger women. I asked why she didn't spend more time with people her own age. She replied, "Son, when you get my age, if you are not making friends with younger people, one day you won't have any friends. Most of my older friends are dead!" Sure enough, when my grandmother was in the nursing home, a parade of younger women visited her regularly.

Old Friends

An old adage says, "New friends are silver; old friends are gold." We should not neglect our old friends. Old friends are like old shoes—comfortable. Again, the Apocrypha has it right: "Do not abandon old friends, for new ones cannot equal them. A new friend is like new wine; when it has aged, you can drink it with pleasure" (Sirach 9:10).

Old friends are friends for all seasons. They know our stories, and we know theirs. We have been witnesses to one another's lives. Between us, there are stories that others do not find interesting, and there are explanations that do not have to be made. When we are around other people, we sometimes feel as if we have a reverse case of amnesia: We constantly have to explain to people who we are. This is not necessary with old friends. They already know who we are.

I have managed to hold on to friendships from every era and port in my life. I thank God for each of these friendships. As I get older, they are more and more important to me.

Because of our sophisticated means of communication, there is no reason to lose touch with old friends. People move, but relocation does not have to mean the loss of a friend. Thomas Jefferson spent up to three hours a day writing letters to his friends. After his death, his grandson found on file copies of sixteen thousand letters he had written.[11] In an age of smartphones, e-mail, texting, and social media, maintaining contact with old friends is much easier than ever before. It is possible to be apart without being separated.

The tragedy is that as time passes, our old friends begin to die. The clock runs out. The death of an old friend brings us grief. It stings to know our friend is gone and will not return. We will never see our friend again in this world. We will never again have a pleasant conversation. Some people say, "Time heals all wounds," but they are incorrect. The wound never closes, the tear never repairs, and the world never goes back to normal. We have lost part of ourselves. We will miss our old friends for as long as we live. We are left to cling to the sacred hope of reunion on the other shore. But in spite of the grief, we realize that having had our friends was well worth the pain.

God would not have created us to be relational if we were incapable of finding and growing friendships. Just as a couch potato can learn to run marathons, so can socially awkward, emotionally aloof persons learn to have close, intimate friendships. Friendship is a learned skill. It may not come naturally to you; other people may be better at it than you are; but you can learn to be relational enough to find fulfillment in friendships. Another verse from the Apocrypha says, "Faithful friends are life-saving medicine; and those who fear, the Lord will find them" (Sirach 6:16). Praise God for that!

CHAPTER 6

Friendship . . . for the Moment or Forever?

"To cement a new friendship...
a spark with which both were secretly charged
must fly from one person to another,
and cut across the accident of place and time."

George Santayana

I am good at dreaming, strategizing, and even getting things started. The hard part is execution. My problem is following through.

What I know about sustaining covenant friendships I learned from two women. Sadly, throughout history, most classical thinkers have considered females incapable of real friendship. It will not surprise anyone to learn that the people who held this viewpoint were male. The truth is that women tend to know more about relationships than men. Social scientists agree that the loneliness of men in Western society is pervasive. Most married men think of their wives as their best friends, even though their wives think of other women as filling this role.[1]

Regardless of which gender we think is better at relationships, one thing is certain: We can all take a lesson from Ruth and Naomi on how to sustain a covenant friendship. Their ancient story, recounted in the book of Ruth in the Bible, is as contemporary as tomorrow's newspaper.

The story begins with Elimelech and Naomi, a Jewish couple from Bethlehem, Judea. Bethlehem means "house of bread." But a famine struck, and there was no bread in the "house of bread." Desperate people will do whatever it takes to survive. Elimelech and Naomi looked at their withering crops and perishing flocks, and they realized starvation was near. So they packed up their meager possessions, including their two sons, and retraced the last part of Israel's exodus journey. They set out for the fertile, well-watered plains of Moab. It was only thirty miles away, but culturally and religiously, the two countries were light-years apart.

In Moab, everything went wrong for Elimelech's family. First, Elimelech died. Next, Naomi's sons married pagan women, which was forbidden by Jewish law (Deuteronomy 7:3–4). Finally, Naomi's two sons died prematurely, before they had an opportunity to give her grandchildren. With no husbands or sons, she was "cut off from the land of the living" (Isaiah 53:8).

The situation for Naomi could not have been worse. Naomi was now widowed, childless, and grandchild-less. She had no one to provide for her and protect her. In addition, she was burdened with two pagan Moabite daughters-in-law. How would the three women survive? Naomi would have to become a beggar.

Finally Naomi caught a break. Word came that the famine in Judea was over. The barley crop in Bethlehem was said to be bountiful. Perhaps she and her two Moabite daughters-in-law could glean enough grain to keep from starving. After all, Jewish law commanded harvesters to leave grain in the corners of the field for "the poor and the immigrants" (Leviticus 19:10). She was poor and her daughters-in-law were immigrants, so they qualified.

The three women set out for Bethlehem, but somewhere along the road, Naomi changed her mind. She decided that her two Moabite daughters-in-law should return to their native land and families. Neither of them knew the language, the customs, or the religion of Judea. They would be misfits in Bethlehem. Why should she be the caretaker for two refugee daughters-in-law? Let their families provide for them.

Naomi gave Orpah and Ruth a blessing. She said something about not having enough years left to birth husbands for them and sent them packing. Orpah kissed her mother-in-law, said good-bye, and returned home. But Ruth "clung" to Naomi.

Clung (Ruth 1:14) is an interesting Hebrew word. It is the same word used to describe the covenant of marriage in Genesis 2:24: "Therefore a man leaves his father and his mother and clings to his wife, and they become one flesh." Clinging is as much emotional and spiritual as it is physical. It is about holding on to a bond. Ruth clung to a bond with Naomi.

The lives of Ruth and Naomi became forever intertwined that day. They were no longer two but one. Note the covenant words Ruth spoke to Naomi:

Do not press me to leave you or turn back from following you! Where you go, I will go; where you lodge, I will lodge; your people shall be my people, and your God my God. Where you die, I will die—there will I be buried. May the Lord do thus and so to me, and more as well, even if death parts me from you (Ruth 1:16–17).

Ruth chose to tie herself permanently to Naomi "for better or for worse." She made a friendship covenant with her. She opted for interdependence instead of independence.

Occasionally I officiate the marriage of someone who wants Ruth 1:16–17 read at their wedding. I always tell them that the proper way to include these words in the service is for the bride to read them to her mother-in-law! This explanation usually kills the request.

When Naomi arrived home in Bethlehem, her old friends greeted her. "Welcome home, Naomi," they said. Naomi responded, "Don't call me Naomi ("sweet") any more. From now on, call me Mara ("bitter") because the Lord has dealt bitterly with me. I left Bethlehem full, and I have returned home empty." Grief had emptied her of hope, and bitterness had swept in to take its place.

Rather than begging for financial assistance, Naomi asked Ruth to go to the field of Boaz, a relative of Elimelech, to glean for food. Naomi was a smart lady. She had more than food in mind. Boaz was an older fellow and a confirmed bachelor. Naomi was thinking matrimony, but she did not explain her strategy to Ruth.

Gleaning was dangerous business. Ruth was an unmarried foreigner. That meant it was very likely she would be raped. Knowing the risk, Ruth did what Naomi suggested anyway.

Boaz noticed Ruth immediately and commanded his employees not to bother her. During the day, Ruth asked Boaz why he had treated her with such courtesy. He answered, "Because of what you are doing for Naomi." There may have been another reason as well. In some ways, Ruth reminded Boaz of his mother. Boaz's mother was Rahab, the Jericho prostitute who had protected the Jewish reconnaissance team Joshua had sent in to spy out the land of promise (Joshua 2:1–21; 6:22–25; Matthew 1:6). Rahab's entire family, which was non-Jewish, had been spared because of her generosity to the Jewish spies.

At the end of the workday, Boaz gave Ruth additional food for her and Naomi. When Ruth got home, she told Naomi all that had happened. Then Naomi explained the family ties between Boaz and Elimelech.

Next, Naomi hatched a daring plan. She helped Ruth to get dolled up and sent her back to the field of Boaz. The plan was for Ruth to sneak into the field after the weary field hands were sleeping and position herself at Boaz's feet—a posture of submission. Pretty forward, right?

It was an incredibly risky scheme. Boaz could have used her sexually and then cast her aside as a prostitute. After all, she was not a virgin. Or he could have left her alone and spread his garment over her, an image of protection. Would it be a one-night stand or a marriage? Naomi was counting on Boaz being attracted to Ruth and being a man of moral character. Ruth didn't have to go along with Naomi's plan, but she chose to. She trusted in the wisdom of Naomi and the integrity of Boaz.

Boaz was amazed that Ruth chose to be with an older man like him instead of one of the younger men who worked for him. He spread his garment over her, and they lay there together in silence until just before the sun rose. Then Boaz sent her home before anyone knew she had been there. He did not want to soil Ruth's reputation. So Naomi's scheme worked out well.

When Ruth got home early that morning, she reported to Naomi all that had happened. Naomi predicted that Boaz would act quickly to claim Ruth as his wife. And that is exactly what he did.

When Boaz married Ruth, he got a two-for-the-price-of-one deal. He got a new wife and his wife's former mother-in-law. He couldn't have Ruth without Naomi because the two women were bonded in covenant friendship.

It wasn't long before Ruth had a baby boy. They called him Obed. Old Naomi became the child's nurse. Naomi later said of Ruth, "She was more to me than seven sons" (Ruth 4:15). Obed became the grandfather of King David. So Ruth, the Jewish convert from Moab, was King David's great-grandmother.

Have you ever known friends like Ruth and Naomi—friends who were so close that it was impossible to think of one without the other? Ruth and Naomi were an unlikely pair. They were unqualified for friendship, according to Aristotle, who said, "The two things that contribute most greatly to friendship are common upbringing and similarity of age."[2] Ruth and Naomi had neither of these two things in common.

Two women friends I know are often mistaken for each other. After decades of being best friends, they act so much alike that people often ask them if they are sisters . . . even twins. The interesting thing about that is this: One is an American Indian-skinned, dark-eyed brunette, while the other is a fair-skinned, blue-eyed natural blonde. It is their covenant friendship that makes them seem so alike.

The story of Ruth and Naomi can teach us a great deal about how to sustain a covenant friendship. Six words, each beginning with an "A," describe their relationship. If we can learn to live by these six relational words, our friendships will flourish.

Allegiance

First, Ruth made an unconditional pledge of allegiance to Naomi. Her unqualified commitment is important to understand, especially because there was such a cultural divide between them. The Spanish writer and philosopher George Santayana made this observation: "To cement a new friendship, especially between foreigners or persons of different social worlds, a spark with which both were secretly charged must fly from one person to another, and cut across the accident of place and time."[3] This spark flew from Ruth to Naomi. Ruth chose to bond to her. She vowed to stick by Naomi no matter what—regardless of difficulties, inconveniences, obstacles, or sacrifices. It was more than an until-death-parts-us promise. Ruth insisted that the two women would be buried together (Ruth 1:16–17).

Ruth's pledge of loyalty would make more sense if she could have known how the story would end. She had no idea she would be the great-grandmother of King David and a relative of Jesus the Messiah (Matthew 1:1–16). If she had followed the conventional wisdom of her day, she would have returned home to the security of Moab, as Orpah had done.

Why would Ruth sign up for such unfavorable terms? She agreed to be poor and homeless. She gave up her family, language, culture, and religion. And she took on the care of a bitter old woman. But in return, Ruth got a covenant friend, and nothing is more valuable than a covenant friend.

Can there be a covenant friendship without a mutually agreed-on covenant? Yes, but presumption can lead to misunderstanding and disappointment. Conversely, the promise of loyalty provides fertile soil in which trust can grow.

Notice that the covenant made by Ruth to Naomi was unilateral. Ruth initiated the covenant by making an oath of loyalty to Naomi. Initially, Naomi made no similar commitment to Ruth. The two women had known each other for several years. They had shared great joy and grief. But Ruth's words must have caught Naomi by surprise. It was only after Naomi had taken time to process the commitment that their covenant became reciprocal. Covenant friendships begin with someone being bold enough to offer a unilateral oath of allegiance to another person.

Covenant oaths are important. Epicurus was right when he observed, "What helps us in friendship is not so much the help our friends give us as the assurance we feel concerning the promise of help."[4]

The offer of friendship must leave the other person free to say, "No thanks" or "Not at this time." We cannot demand that people accept our offer of covenant friendship. We can only make the offer and patiently wait for their response.

Many years ago, I went to lunch with a businessman in Lubbock, Texas. In the middle of the meal, he said to me, "Jim, you are my brother."

I responded, "Yes, we are all brothers."

"No, Jim," he persisted, "you have not understood me. I have two brothers. One lives in Lamesa, and you are my other brother."

It took me awhile to absorb that he was making a unilateral commitment to me. He was adopting me as a brother. But before long, I began to view him as an adopted brother and covenant friend. Many years have passed since we shared that lunch. I no longer live in West Texas, but our friendship continues. His pledge of allegiance proved to be genuine. And I hope mine has as well.

Will you give the gift of allegiance to a friend?

Acceptance

Second, Ruth accepted Naomi as she was. Friendship means we can be authentically who we are in the relationship and allow others to be who they are at the same time. Ruth gave that kind of gift of acceptance to Naomi.

Naomi had once been an optimistic person. As noted earlier, the name *Naomi* meant "sweet." But her three devastating losses had shipwrecked her life. Now she was "bitter" (Ruth 1:20). Ruth, on the other hand, had a hopeful, future-oriented perspective on life. What was it that Ruth saw in Naomi that made her want to cling to her? I believe it was the reality of God that Ruth had seen in Naomi through the years, in spite of her unresolved grief.

The only way two people can have an enduring friendship is for both of them to recognize but choose to look past each other's flaws, faults, and foibles. When we enter a covenant with people, we agree to accept them as they are. Acceptance does not mean we necessarily agree with them or approve of what they do. It is a decision to love them regardless of what they do. And they do the same for us. Peter wrote, "Love covers a multitude of sins" (1 Peter 4:8).

When we try to fix people, they experience our rejection. They hear us saying, "I find you unacceptable the way you are, but if you change, I will love you." Rather than drawing people to us, it drives them away. No one wants to be someone else's project. Guy Greenfield wrote, "The quickest way to destroy a budding relationship is to set in to convert or change the other to fit some preconceived notion."[5]

Two covenant friends I know have owned a house together for more than twenty years. One lives upstairs; one lives downstairs. One is a left-brained, business-oriented, highly organized person. The other is a right-brained, highly creative, not-so-organized person. They have survived (and thrived) as friends and housemates by agreeing to a special arrangement. The common areas of the house—living room, dining room, kitchen, library, and guest room—are kept neat and clean, but each person may keep their own areas—bedrooms, baths, and offices—any way they want. They have accepted each other's gifts, limitations, and natural tendencies. And it works.

Jesus was called "a friend of tax collectors and sinners" (Matthew 11:19). He said to spiritual outsiders, "You belong!" Jesus didn't just tolerate them; he accepted them. Acceptance is not earned; it is a gift.

First John 4:18 says, "Fear has to do with judgment." Judgment is the feeling of being evaluated, of having someone measure us to see whether or not we are acceptable. We experience fear when we sense people are judging us in this way. John adds, "Perfect love casts out fear." When we see the word love in the New Testament, we can substitute the words *accept* or *acceptance*. When people know they are accepted as they are, fear evaporates.

I love Colorado and the Rocky Mountains, but those majestic peaks look better at a distance than they do up close. When you get to the top, you discover that the spaces that look so breathtaking at a distance are actually bald, rocky, and barren. The same is true with people. From a distance, people appear to have their acts together, but when you get up close, you can see their deficiencies and inconsistencies. All people have clay feet. If acceptance requires perfection, no one will ever qualify.

It is acceptance that makes it possible for friends to take off their masks and become real with us. We cannot risk revealing our true selves until we know we will be accepted as we are. Paul wrote, "Accept one another just as Christ has accepted you, for the glory of God" (Romans 15:7).

Will you give the gift of acceptance to a friend?

Availability

Third, Ruth made herself available to Naomi. Ruth said to her former mother-in-law, "Where you go, I will go; where you lodge, I will lodge. Where you die I will die" (Ruth 1:16–17). Ruth made a covenant to do life with Naomi—to be available to her. Friends make this same decision when they say to each other, "You can count on me. I will be there for you." Proverbs 17:17 says, "A friend loves at all times."

The importance of a ministry of presence cannot be overstated. When we are in emotional pain and cry out, "Why?" God does not give us the academic answer we request. God gives us what we need—a sense of the divine presence. Psalm 145:18 says, "The Lord is near to all who call on him."

Likewise, when friends make themselves available to us, even if no words are spoken, it is incredibly strengthening. Their presence says, "I am with you. I care." Isn't that why we make a special effort to attend people's baptisms, weddings, birthdays, anniversaries, and graduations? Isn't that why we visit our friends who are sick, hospitalized, and shut in?

Busyness is therefore a primary barrier to covenant friendship. Busyness causes us to focus on urgent trivia rather than important people. In order to be available for our friends, we have to put them high on our priority lists, sacrificing other things that people who demand our time and energy.

Somewhere I read a story about two high school friends who signed up for military duty under a "buddy plan." They went through basic training and fought together in Vietnam. One day, while on patrol, they were pinned down by enemy fire. Mortars and artillery filled the sky like fireworks on the Fourth of July. One of the two young men lay wounded, unable to move. The sergeant called for the unit to retreat, leaving the wounded soldier temporarily behind. Ignoring the order, his friend plunged ahead to the place the young man's body rested. Though wounded in the process of retrieving his friend, the soldier mustered the strength to pick his friend up and drag him back to the unit. By the time they reached safety, it was apparent that the fallen soldier was dead.

In anger, the sergeant asked the rescuing comrade, "Well, was it worth it?"

The soldier replied, "Yes, sir, it was. When I got to him, he said, 'I knew you'd come.'"

As I write this story, my mind is reviewing my history. I am recalling the people who have been there for me during my hours of need. They rearranged their priorities to practice a "ministry of presence." I remember a friend who sought me out when my grandmother died. I was hiding like a wounded animal. It required some effort to find me. He walked up to me, gave me a bear hug, then turned around and walked away. He never said a word, but his caring presence brought me great strength that day. And the memory of his love sustains me today, even though he is in heaven.

Will you give the gift of availability to a friend?

Affirmation

Fourth, Ruth affirmed Naomi on an ongoing basis. When Ruth made a covenant with Naomi, her former mother-in-law was a bitter person (Ruth 1:20). As time passed, she became herself again—"sweet" Naomi. What brought about this transformation? The Scripture writer says it was the love of her daughter-in-law, Ruth, who was "better than seven sons" to her (Ruth 4:15).

An important way of being good covenant companions is speaking words of affirmation to our friends. Most of us hear far too much negativity. There are always people eager to criticize, complain, and condemn. We might well change the line in "Home on the Range" to "where seldom is heard an encouraging word." We desperately need friends who will counteract the prevailing currents and speak encouraging words to us.

When I was a child, undiagnosed dyslexia made it difficult for me to read. Many times, in an effort to keep from being discovered as a nonreader, I was disruptive in school. Whenever we took turns reading, I would look ahead at the paragraph I would likely be assigned to read. When my projection of where we would be when it came time for me to read was inaccurate, I would often create a disturbance to keep from being exposed as a nonreader. One day in the third grade, when I had been sent to the hall for having disturbed the peace, my teacher, Ms. Smith, who was also my neighbor and Sunday school teacher, came out and spoke to me. Rather than shaming me, she said, "Jim, one day you are going to do wonderful things, and we will all be so proud of you. Now go on back into the room and don't throw any more spitballs." For many years, I held on to Ms. Smith's affirmation.

There are at least three forms of affirmation each of us needs to hear.

A New Name

An important form of affirmation is naming. Jesus gave his closest friends new names. He called Simon "Rocky" (Peter);

he referred to James and John as "the Thunderbolt Brothers" (Sons of Thunder). These nicknames were not insults but Jesus' declarations of faith in them. Jesus believed in them more than they believed in themselves. He was saying to them, "Peter, I see you as a person who can become as solid as a rock, and James and John, you're as strong as thunderbolts."

We see in our friends more than they have thus far evidenced. And we use positive names and affirming words for them related more to their potential than their past performance. Ms. Smith said to me, "I see you as a person who can be worthwhile."

Encouragement

Encouragement is another form of affirmation. Words are powerful—much more powerful than we realize. Successful corporate CEOs are expert communicators. Their job description is to cast a vision so compelling that it draws the resources necessary to fulfill the vision. People fall in love and get married because words are spoken and vows are exchanged. Words have the power to create—and the power to destroy. We should speak words to our friends that will create rather than destroy. Jesus said that when words are spoken, they do not vanish. They stick around and build things up and destroy things. He said that one day we will be held accountable for all our words (Matthew 12:37).

When Mary, Jesus' mother, became pregnant, she went to see Elizabeth, her cousin. Rather than questioning Mary's integrity or saying, "Shame on you," Elizabeth exclaimed, "Blessed are you among women, and blessed is the fruit of your womb!" (Luke 1:42). How healing these words must have been to Mary.

Paul wrote, "Let no evil talk come out of your mouth, but only what is useful to build up, as there is need, so that your words may give grace to those who hear" (Ephesians 4:29). The writer of Hebrews puts it this way: "Let us consider how to provoke one another to love and good deeds" (10:24).

My teacher chose to speak words of encouragement rather than condemnation to me. And her words are still a source of affirmation.

Remembering

A third form of affirmation is remembering. Some wise person said, "A friend is someone who knows the song of our heart and when we have forgotten the words or the tune, sings it to us again and again until we can sing it again for ourselves." It is easy for the circumstances of life to uproot us. Amnesia sets in. We forget who we are and what our dreams are. We need a covenant friend who will help us learn to sing the song of our heart again.

Time and time again, I have needed the ministry of remembering from friends. Every advanced degree I have earned has been because of the encouragement of rememberers. Hopefully I have given this ministry to others as well.

Carolyn has a dear friend named Ginger. But Ginger suffers from bipolar disorder. Carolyn once asked Ginger, "When you're in your depressed state, what can I do to help?"

Ginger said, "When I'm lost in my depression, I forget who I am and what I can do. You need to remind me."

The next time Ginger fell into serious depression, Carolyn wrote her a five-page, handwritten letter reminding Ginger that she is a brilliant decorator and designer, wears hats with great flair as no one else can, is a wonderful singer, and is a beautiful friend.

Friends remember our good traits, even when we forget. Will you give the gift of affirmation to a friend?

Attention

Fifth, Ruth was attentive to Naomi. When Ruth made a covenant with Naomi, she promised to keep her mother-in-law on her radar screen—to love her, stand beside her, serve her, and provide for her. Ruth was faithful to the covenant. She did not forsake her friend (Proverbs 27:10). She gave Naomi the attention her oath necessitated.

Attention is not looking after our friends just when they are in crisis. It is ordinary, everyday concern for their best interests (Philippians 2:4). Attentiveness requires careful observation and consistent care. But attentiveness does not go beyond the bounds of necessity, creating a sense of obligation in our friend.

Do you know why so many people are reluctant to commit to a friendship covenant? It is because friendship counteracts our contemporary addiction to comfort and convenience! Like the story Jesus told, sometimes our friends show up at inconvenient times, needing things from us (Luke 11:5–8).

I admire the comment a friend made about a mutual friend years ago: "If you are going through a hard time, save your last quarter because you are going to need it to call our friend. Because when you call him, he will come." We all need to be that kind of friend!

Paul gives us this exhortation: "Now concerning love of the brothers and sisters, you do not need to have anyone write to you, for you yourselves have been taught by God to love one another; indeed you do love all the brothers and sisters . . . but I urge you, beloved, to do so more and more" (1 Thessalonians 4:9–10).

Will you give the gift of attention to a friend?

Accountability

And sixth, the covenant Ruth entered made her accountable to Naomi. When we enter a covenant friendship, we surrender the right to secrecy about areas in our lives that are damaged or out of control. We opt for intimacy over privacy.

Jesus said, "For where two or three gather in my name, there am I with them" (Matthew 18:20). Many of the older translations used to say "two or more," which could include thousands of people. That would mean this teaching would be equivalent to Jesus' great commission promise to be with us always (Matthew 28:20). But Matthew 18:20 seems to imply something far more intimate and demanding. It promises that when we gather in Jesus' name in transparency and accountability, Jesus is with us.

Covenant friends invite each other into their private worlds. Our friends alone know the inner workings of our souls. Only they know the embarrassing truths that we prefer to keep hidden from public view. Mark Twain was reported to have said, "We are all like the moon; we all have a dark side." Covenant friends know our darkness.

I once knew four businessmen who met at 4:30 every morning more than over thirty years to play dominoes. It was not until one of them died that I discovered it was really a closed AA meeting. The playing of dominoes was a cover for their real purpose—to talk candidly about what was going on in their business and family lives and to be held accountable for their Achilles' heel.

Accountability is a familiar concept. Most of us are accountable to others. At work we are accountable to employers, managers, or a board of directors. At home we are accountable to our spouses and other family members. Friendship accountability is similar, except that it involves the revelation of deeply personal and sometimes shameful things.

Accountability is not imposed on us by covenant friends. It is a choice we make. Without accountability, there is no covenant friendship. We give our friends the right to ask us hard questions. And we promise to answer their questions honestly. We agree not to avoid them, deceive them, or lie to them.

There is an old AA saying that goes like this: "The problem is not the problem; hiding the problem is the problem." The New Testament teaches us, "Confess your faults to one another"

(James 5:16). Instead of concealing things, friends reveal them. Rather than denying things, friends disclose them. Friendship is born the moment we come out and disclose the truth about ourselves and they respond, "I thought I was the only one who felt that way . . . struggled with that problem."

George Barna suggests, "Fewer than one out of six churched believers have a relationship with another believer through which spiritual accountability is provided."[6] Barna probably overestimates this percentage. The tragedy is that 100 percent of the people who fall into self-destructive patterns do not have a person to whom they are responsible.

The story is always the same. A bad behavior or an inappropriate relationship begins to develop, and it becomes more and more difficult to stop. In fact, it strengthens and gains momentum. After a while, self-discipline is not enough to curb the habit. All the time, we carry on as if everything was just fine. We keep what is happening well hidden.

There are some stubborn patterns in our lives that will not go away by means of private prayer. The reason is because the problem is rooted in shame. It takes another person who knows what is happening and is committed to hold our feet to the fire to help us break free.

Over and over, the book of Proverbs teaches us that accountability makes it less likely that we will stumble into moral error:

- Proverbs 11:14: "In the abundance of counselors there is safety."
- Proverbs 13:10: "Wisdom is with those who take advice."
- Proverbs 13:18: "One who heeds reproof is honored."
- Proverbs 15:31: "The ear that heeds wholesome admonition will lodge among the wise."
- Proverbs 27:5–6: "Better is open rebuke than hidden love. Well meant are the wounds a friend inflicts."

- Proverbs 28:23: "Whoever rebukes a person will afterwards find more favor than one who flatters with the tongue."

The cardinal rule of accountability is confidentiality. Our covenant friends must be able to unburden their hearts with us in confidence that what they say will never be repeated—to anyone—ever.

Seven Accountability Questions

Charles Swindoll has seven questions he and his staff members must answer weekly in community:

1. Have you been with a member of the opposite sex this past week in a way that might be seen as compromising?
2. Have any of your financial dealings lacked integrity?
3. Have you exposed yourself to sexually explicit material?
4. Have you spent adequate time in Bible study and prayer?
5. Have you given priority time to your family?
6. Have you fulfilled the mandates of your calling?
7. Have you just lied to me?[9]

Will you give the gift of accountability to a friend? Will you receive it from a friend? Who is the right friend to hold you accountable? How often should you meet with that friend? How soon can you get started?

Ruth and Naomi sustained their covenant friendship through allegiance, acceptance, availability, affirmation, attention, and accountability. Will you commit to finding a friend and making these six characteristics part of your friendship covenant?

CHAPTER 7

Friendship Fatality

"I do not have friends; I take prisoners."

From an Alcoholics Anonymous Meeting

This may be the most important chapter in the book. It is the necessary counterbalance to everything I have written up to this point. Let me begin with a confession: I have a long history of struggles with codependency.

Codependency is an occupational hazard for people in the helping professions, such as teachers, physicians, nurses, counselors, or pastors. When people call for help, it is easier to rescue than to listen and prayerfully meditate on the appropriate way to respond. After a while, rescuing becomes a reflex action. And often, as with other forms of codependency, helping professionals who respond soonest are thought to be the best at their job.

My codependent tendencies predate my call to the ministry by many years. I think I know the origins of difficulties. When my father died, my mother's mother came to live with us, to care for my siblings and me while Mother worked. Throughout my growing-up years, she made the same speech to me dozens of times: "Son, you are the man of the house. Your mother and I are counting on your taking care of us when you get older." Her words were encoded in my emotional DNA. I carried Grandmother's words as an obligation well into adulthood. They became a baseline for my understanding of success and failure.

As time passed, I took on new obligations, familial and pastoral. By the time I reached midlife, I had been moderately successful at looking after everyone but myself. It brought on a predictable midlife crisis for which I am now grateful. I was angry at everyone else for a while. But after a period of time, I realized I was actually angry with myself for failing to be the savior of the world. When you go through a crisis, it gives you an opportunity to rethink things. As a result of the crisis, I made a conscious decision to withdraw from messiahship.

Maybe codependency is my issue and not yours. I hope so. But my guess is that what I have to say in this chapter is relevant for most of you as well. Do not let denial cheat you out of a message God has for you.

There is an odd story in the fourteenth chapter of Acts that reflects the pagan culture in which it took place. Two missionaries, Barnabas and Paul, were passing through Lystra, a city that today is in central Turkey. They encountered a fellow who had never walked; he was crippled from birth. Paul saw something in the man that could allow him to respond in faith. So Paul said to him, "Get up!" The guy stood and walked for the first time.

You can imagine the community excitement that followed. Someone pointed to Paul and Barnabas and said, "Zeus and Hermes are here!"

Zeus was the king of all the mythical gods in the Greek pantheon. Legend said he was physically imposing and handsome. Tradition says Barnabas was a tall, handsome fellow.

He was also the leader of the missionary team. Evidently the citizens of Lystra associated Barnabas with Zeus.

Hermes was not as important a god as Zeus. Legend says he was not as handsome, but he was a better speaker. In their minds, he was the messenger god for the other Greek deities. Since tradition says Paul was not physically attractive but was the group spokesman, we can surmise that the Lystrians took Paul to be Hermes.

The town citizens were paying Barnabas and Paul a great compliment. They were saying that these two men were deities. How else could the healing of the crippled man be explained?

Suddenly there was a parade. The citizens were cheering, whooping, and hollering. Why should there not be a community hoopla? Two Greek gods had shown up—not spiritually but in the flesh. The local priest of Zeus got involved in the celebration. He brought an ox so there could be a sacrifice.

When Barnabas and Paul realized what was happening, they stopped the parade and said, "Wait a minute! We are not gods! We are only humans, common folks like you!" But in spite of their strong objection, "They scarcely restrained the crowd from offering sacrifice to them" (Acts 14:18).

What does a story about first-century pagan superstition have to do with contemporary friendship? When we get involved in relationships, there is something in us that can easily get confused. If we are not careful, we can start treating people as though they are gods, expecting of them things that are impossible for them and not good for us. It is a relational phenomenon called "codependency." Codependency did not come into existence in 1976, when the term was coined by addiction experts. It has existed since the beginning of time.

If detachment is a problem for some of us, enmeshment is a problem for others. We latch on to people, becoming possessive of them. We need them, and they need us. We are uneasy about being separated from them. We are terrified of losing them. That kind of extreme dependence and possessiveness is not friendship. It is codependency.

Codependency is an attachment malfunction. We are improperly bonded. We serve the needs of others to satisfy our own egos. What looks like love is actually narcissism. In codependency, there is a lack of healthy self-care and separateness. In her classic book on the subject, Melody Beattie makes a case that codependency occurs when one person is controlled and the other person is controlling.[1]

Codependency is a dark form of spirituality. It is one person making someone other than God their ultimate source—someone other than Jesus their Messiah—and the other person not assuming enough responsibility for their life. It is a dark spirituality that is usually called idolatry. As time passes, it usually becomes more and more compulsive.

That is why Barnabas and Paul became party poopers. They knew that what was happening was more than a case of mistaken identity. It was a spiritual problem. If Barnabas and Paul were gods, then God could not be God. If they were messiahs, then Jesus, whom they had come to proclaim, could not be the Messiah.

Scripture teaches that there are two orders of reality: the created and the uncreated. The created is dependent on and draws its life from the uncreated. The uncreated is contingent on nothing. It is self-existent. Only one thing is uncreated—God. Everything else that exists, including each of us, is on the created side of the ledger.

It is easy for us to become hyper-responsible for other people—to become their Messiah substitute. It flatters our egos to play the role of an all-sufficient provider, to feel as if we know what is best for others and to be in control. Codependent controllers say to other people, "God loves you, and I have a wonderful plan for your life." A friend of mine is fond of saying, "A friend takes an interest in you, but not a controlling one."

Jesus taught that there would be "false Messiahs" (Mark 13:22). False Messiahs are unsafe people. They assume responsibilities they are unable to fulfill. Is it possible that we can become part of the fulfillment of Jesus' negative prophecy? I believe we can.

Likewise, it is easy for us to become hyper-dependent on people—to see them as our Messiah. We get hooked on playing the subservient receiver role because it makes us feel secure to know we have someone to look after us. Alcoholics Anonymous teaches, "Codependents always tell their pushers what they want to hear."

Codependent people have a victim mentality. They do not trust in their ability to handle their own affairs. They fear being inadequate. When the prodigal son returned home from the far country, he said to his father, "I don't want the responsibility of being a son any more. Make me a hired hand, one of your dependents" (Luke 15:19).

When someone who feels compelled to play the role of Messiah gets connected to someone else who wants to be a Messiah—we have codependent enmeshment. Codependency is like a drowning person clutching a non-swimmer.

Codependency Is . . .

- one person over-functioning and the other under-functioning
- one person over-committed and the other under-committed
- one person over-responsible and the other under-responsible
- one person a caretaker and the other a care receiver
- one person a martyr and the other a victim
- one person a fixer and the other wanting to be fixed
- one person a rescuer and the other needing to be rescued
- one person a giver and the other a taker
- one person domineering and the other dependent

- one person the enabler and the other the enabled
- one person grandiose and the other helpless
- one person strong and the other weak
- one person controlling and the other controlled
- one person the parent and the other the child
- one person a savior and the other needing to be saved

Sometimes we paste spiritual words over our codependency to make us feel better about it. We call it charity, service, therapy, ministry, marriage, parenting, friendship. Rather than being helpful, it perpetuates a dysfunctional, unhealthy relationship. It makes both people weaker. And worst of all, it prevents Jesus from being the Messiah.

Codependency happens when "two become one" in an unhealthy way. Instead of becoming brothers or sisters, we become Siamese twins. We are possessive of one another. We depend on one another for too many needs. We have minimal need for other relationships. We are unable to develop an identity separate from the other person. We cannot think of life apart from one another. The relationship is ingrown and unhealthy. If the person with whom we are codependent attempts to break away and form a separate life, we will do everything possible to change that person's mind—cry, threaten, act out, even create emergencies.

We all have strengths, but we also have weaknesses. Here is a rule of thumb: No one is as strong or as weak as we think they are.

Barnabas and Paul would have nothing to do with the Lystran idolatry. Paul saw faith in the crippled man. He believed the man could somehow make direct contact with the Messiah. So he said to the man, "Get up!" Paul did not raise him to his feet. He did not start a home for crippled Lystrians. He spoke challenging words to the man, and the crippled man responded on his own with faith in the Messiah, Jesus.

When the rich young ruler decided against paying the cost of discipleship, Jesus did not run after him or lower the terms to suit him (Mark 10:17–23). Jesus treated him as a morally free agent and respected his decision to walk away. Jesus did not become codependent with him.

Over and over, when Jesus performed miracles, he said to the recipient, "Your faith made you well" (Matthew 9:22; Mark 5:34; 10:52; Luke 8:48; 17:19; 18:42). In other words, real faith is a healthy collaboration between our action and God's actions—between our being responsible for our lives and the Messiah being the Messiah. No faith, no miracle.

You may ask, "Was the friendship of Ruth and Naomi codependent?" No, Naomi turned Ruth loose, and Ruth made a decision not to leave. Their relationship was mutual.

I often find myself in situations when I do not know what to do. I can't tell whether what I am encountering is my responsibility or someone else's. In those situations, I prayerfully ask myself this question: "Is this about me, or is this about them?" If it is about me, I need to do something about it. If it is about them, they need to do something about it. It is not helpful to meet needs for people that they can and should meet for themselves.

Now let me bring the point home specifically to friendship. Jesus points out that covenant friends must be willing to lay down their lives for each other (John 15:13). But if the friendship becomes codependent, then the relationship is unbalanced. One person carries an unbearable burden, and the other person becomes irresponsible. Then the ties that bind us are putting one person in a bind and permitting the other person to go free.

How do we engage in covenant friendships without becoming codependent? According to addiction specialists, a large percentage of us have a propensity to unequal, unhealthy, one-sided, codependent relationships. We tend to fall into the same relational traps time and time again. But there are ways to avoid these snares and opt for healthy friendships. It is my hope that the balance of this chapter will make a small contribution toward helping us make good relational choices.

Paul offers us two helpful relational insights in the sixth chapter of his letter to the churches of Galatia. He wrote this:

- "Bear one another's burdens and so fulfill the law of Christ" (Galatians 6:2).
- "For all must carry their own load" (Galatians 6:5).

Paul was saying that in healthy relationships, we are able to say two seemingly opposite things to our covenant friends:

"I Am Responsible"

What did Paul mean when he wrote, "Bear one another's burden and so fulfill the law of Christ" (Galatians 6:2)? He meant that there are times when all of us have loads larger than we can carry. We need a friend to come alongside us and get under the load with us. Notice that it is "get under the load with us," not "get under the load for us." The Greek word used here for "burden" refers to "an overwhelming load too great for us to bear alone."

The parable of the Good Samaritan makes the same point. Jesus makes the point that good neighbors seek to meet the needs of people in their sphere of influence that they cannot meet by themselves. The man on the Jericho Road was robbed and half-dead. He was not able to bandage his wounds, get to medical assistance, or pay the bill (Luke 10:33–35). The Good Samaritan's compassion led him to meeting needs that the beaten man could not meet by himself. The Good Samaritan was not an enabler.

Paul's reference to "the law of Christ" (Galatians 6:2) is the law of love. In an earlier passage in the same letter, Paul quoted Jesus and the Bible: "You shall love your neighbor as yourself" (Galatians 5:14; Mark 12:31; Leviticus 19:18). When we are under a crushing burden, and a friend helps us to carry it, the friend is fulfilling "the law of Christ."

Paul gave us a practical illustration of what kind of loads we are responsible for helping our friends carry: "My friends, if anyone is detected in a transgression, you who have received the Spirit should restore such a one in a spirit of gentleness. Take care that you yourself are not tempted . . . For when those who are nothing think they are something, they deceive themselves" (Galatians 6:1, 3). These words deserve a careful explanation.

Detected

The word *detected* implies that we spiritually discern that something is going wrong in our friend's life. We sense that there is a problem, even though no one may have told us. We take note of a change in their attitude or behavior. We observe the shifts that only someone intimately related to them could see. Or perhaps what we detect is revealed to us supernaturally. God somehow drops an insight about the friend into our conscious mind through intuition, meditation, or a dream. Suddenly we have a flash of insight about our friend.

Some Bible translations use the word *overtaken* rather than *detected*. The image the word *overtaken* implies is evil pursuing us. When it overtakes us, it is because we have failed to run fast enough from evil. The Bible warns us to flee from evil (1 Corinthians 6:18; 10:14; 1 Timothy 6:11; 2 Timothy 2:22). How, then, do we become overtaken by sin? We do not take the temptation seriously enough. We fail to be on guard against it. We flirt with it. We do not turn to God for help, so it nabs us.

Transgression

A transgression is going somewhere you are not supposed to go, doing something you are not supposed to do, or saying something you are not supposed to say. It is disregarding the no-trespassing signs God has posted in our hearts. The result of transgression is harm to a person's life.

Restore

What is our responsibility to friends who cross the line and start down the wrong road? Paul says we are to "detect" the "transgression" and seek to "restore" them (Galatians 6:1).

The Greek word translated as "restore" is the same word used for setting a broken bone or putting a dislocated joint back in place. When our friends are broken by their violations of God's law, we are to seek to mend them, to repair them, to restore them. This spiritual responsibility is often called "intervention" in the Twelve Step realm.

The work of restoration Paul has in mind is personal and private. We are to go to the person directly, not discuss the matter with a third party. Involving third parties is called "triangulation." The Bible calls it "gossip" (Proverbs 11:13; 20:19). Either way, it creates dysfunction.

The word *restore* in Galatians 6:1 is in the present active tense. We are not to seek to restore the person once and then forget it. We are to work at restoration continuously. We must intervene time and time again. The restoration of a friend is likely to be a long-term process.

We all need a friend who cares about us so much that he or she will not allow us to go down the wrong road without standing on our path and attempting to turn us around. That person is willing to do this even if the intervention is not appreciated, and it means risking the future of the friendship. Frankly I have lost a friend or two along the way through restoration efforts. Not everyone who needs help wants it or will accept it. Since we are choosing not to be codependent, we ultimately have to let them go.

Who Have Received the Spirit

Paul said the ones who do this ministry should be the ones who "have received the Spirit" or those who "have a spiritual perspective on life" (Galatians 6:1). In other words, we are to depend not on ourselves but on the Holy Spirit for this work of restoration. What instinct is to an animal, the Holy Spirit is to us.

A Spirit of Gentleness

Paul is saying that restoration must be done with "a spirit of gentleness" (Galatians 6:1). Earlier in his letter to the Galatians, Paul had referred to "gentleness" as a fruit of the Holy Spirit (Galatians 5:23).

Why is gentleness necessary? It is because people are more fragile than they appear. They are like china dolls, easily broken. Paul said, "We have this treasure in clay jars" (2 Corinthians 4:7). We can say and do things that will injure our friends. So our words and deeds must be well chosen, gracious, and gentle.

It is always best to ask questions rather than to make accusations. There is no place for anger, harshness, blaming, faultfinding, or criticism. We are to be gentle as Jesus was.

Deceive Themselves

Paul goes on to warn us of self-deception. He writes, "Take care that you yourself are not tempted . . . For when those who are nothing think they are something, they deceive themselves" (Galatians 6:1, 3). Deception is bad, but the worst kind of deception is self-deception. It is easy to become self-deceived, to be in denial, to think we are okay when we are not, to be tempted and not know it. We must become aware of our weaknesses. Otherwise, transgressions will enter our lives through these vulnerabilities. The problems we see clearly in others we do not see in ourselves. And many times, they are the same problems! We are trying to kill our own demons, and we do not even know it. We are attempting to fix in others what is broken in us. Psychologists call it "projection."

But even when our problems are different from our friend's problems, it is hypocritical not to face the person honestly. Before we try to help someone else, we should take a long, hard look at ourselves. Jesus said, "First take the log out of your eye, and then you will see clearly to take the speck out of your neighbor's eye" (Matthew 7:5).

When spiritual people, who are aware of and have dealt with their weaknesses, detect that a friend has gone off course, they are supernaturally able to gently do the work of restoration. I know because the work of non-codependent restoration has been done for me.

Several years ago, I experienced severe burnout. I was physically, emotionally, and spiritually exhausted. My adrenal glands had been overworked for so long they were in rebellion. My whole life was off balance. One night at 9:30 p.m., two friends showed up at my house. They said, "Do you realize how tired you are?"

I answered honestly, "I think so."

Then they went for the kill. "We are here," they exclaimed, "to ask you to leave town and go for an extended period of rest."

I protested, "I would love to, but it is impossible. Look at my calendar. It is filled with appointments, speaking engagements, weddings, funerals, meetings, and commitments of every sort."

Then one of them asked a troubling question: "Do you have anything left to give to all those people?"

The question stunned me. Finally I answered honestly, "No, I don't."

They continued their gentle intervention until I agreed to leave town immediately, not even waiting for the sun to rise. They took responsibility for finding suitable substitutes for all my obligations. I spent several weeks in rest and recuperation. The loving confrontation of two friends helped to restore me.

Something similar happened several years later. A close friend died, and I was not dealing with it well. Grief had knocked my life off course. Two other friends showed up in my office, asking me to leave immediately for a period of R&R. Again I took their advice, and the result was restoration.

Make no mistake about it. There is a sense in which we are responsible for our friends. But the opposite is also true. There is a sense in which we are not responsible for them!

"I Am Not Responsible"

Aelred of Rievaulx argued that because Jesus taught his apostles to lay down their lives for one another (John 15:13), it followed that "nothing should be denied to a friend."[2] I beg to differ.

Yes, we are to lay down our lives for our friends, but does that mean we should indiscriminately cosign bank notes, loan money, and allow people to move in with us? Do the words of Jesus mean we are to have no boundaries? No! Sometimes our rescuing creates big problems:

- We weaken the people we are trying to help.
- We change the nature of the friendship.
- We prevent people from learning lessons God has for them.

Through the years, I have heard hundreds of recovery stories in AA meetings. I have never once heard anyone tell about being rescued over and over and it leading to sobriety. But I have heard many people tell about having people stop rescuing them, coming to the end of themselves, and finding God and sobriety at the bottom. In fact, rescuers have often been the thing that kept these people from hitting bottom, finding God, and sobriety! These rescuers mean well, but their actions are counterproductive.

In contrast, Paul said emphatically that we must know when to say to our friends, "I am not responsible for you. I will not take care of you. I set you free. You are on your own." Paul's own words were, "For all must carry their own load" (Galatians 6:5). He tells us to say "no" to the part of us that wants to do more than we should do. Codependents have a warped sense of responsibility. We need Paul's correction in order to detach from our unhealthy urges.

Wait a minute: Are verse 2 ("bear one another's burdens") and verse 5 ("all must carry their own load") contradictory? No, the words *burden* in verse 2 and *load* in verse 5 refer to two different kinds of responsibilities. A burden is something overwhelming and far too great to carry alone. Load refers to the general obligations and inevitable pressures everyone has. Each one of us must shoulder our own everyday loads. My mother used to say, "Maturity is learning to do the things that need to be done, when they need to be done, whether you feel like doing them or not."

Why would it be necessary for Paul to urge everyone to "carry their own load"? (Galatians 6:5). It is because codependency has always been a struggle in the Christian community. Codependency is a relational disease that afflicts good, generous, gracious folks. It is contracted by people who are loving, kind-hearted, and servant-spirited. Somehow these people tend to love too much, give too much, and serve too much. What looks like love from a distance is codependency when you look at it up close. It is about allowing someone other than Jesus to be the Messiah, or assuming the place of the Messiah for others and thereby replacing Jesus.[2]

The wonderful thing about having Jesus rather than someone or something else as our Messiah is that Jesus never rules over us. He is our Lord, but he does not lord it over us. He does not dominate or control us. He doesn't force us to do things. Instead, he liberates us, giving us free will (John 8:36). When Jesus is our Lord, we become free for the first time.

Many of the people who claim Jesus as their Messiah and Lord (Romans 10:9; 1 Corinthians 12:3; Philippians 2:11) are actually ruled by hurtful memories and controlling people. It is not Jesus but twisted emotions and relationships that control them.

Healthy friendship occurs when we, like Jesus, set one another free—free to have boundaries, to have other relationships, to make different choices. We set them free from us. Friendships are freeing, not enslaving. This is why codependency dooms true friendships.

In order to help us determine whether we have assumed the place of the Messiah for someone else, or allowed someone other than Jesus to become our Messiah, we should ask ourselves two questions:

Do I Feel Responsible for Carrying Loads That Are Not Mine?

False Messiahs easily slip into the roles of rescuer, caretaker, help-aholic, protector, provider, fixer, hero, and martyr. Playing these roles makes us feel important. We get hooked on the need to be needed. According to Carmen Renee Berry, codependents live on the basis of two mottos:

1. "If I don't do it, it won't get done."[3] The folks in AA call this "grandiosity." People who live by this motto are doomed to spreading themselves out too thinly and end up exhausted and cynical.
2. "Everybody else's needs take priority over mine."[4] While trying to take care of others, codependents neglect themselves and ignore their own needs. Sometimes they actually forget that they have needs. Rather than taking care of themselves, these people give to others what they need to receive themselves. Why don't they take care of themselves? Because they have been programmed to think it is a selfish and un-Christian thing to do. They think they are supposed to practice perpetual self-denial. When Jesus said, "Deny yourself" (Mark 8:34), he was not urging us to neglect our being or our core needs.

Many people who grew up in the church were taught the JOY principle. We were told our life priorities should be, "Jesus first, others second, and yourself last." The problem with the JOY principle is that it leaves us without joy and feeling guilty. It tyrannizes our lives. It turns us into workaholics and false Messiahs. Sometimes the most Christian thing we can do is to release the other person and look after ourselves. The good news is that if we resign as people's Messiah, they might discover Jesus, the true Messiah.

Do I Expect Other People to Carry My Load?

People who are looking for someone to look after them, to solve their problems, to be responsible for them, always get connected to other people who need to be caretakers. Likewise, codependent people who want someone to take care of them will always find another codependent who needs to be needed. Hosts always find a parasite, and parasites always find hosts.

Pastors are often the worst codependents of all. We mainline on being needed and find it difficult to say no. When we encounter people who are playing the role of helpless victims, we can't help ourselves. We treat all these people as though they were the man beaten and left half-dead on the Jericho Road (Luke 10:25–37). Pastors sometimes even teach laypeople to be dependent on them. Rather than helping laypeople to become mature believers who can care for themselves, pastors subconsciously keep them immature and dependent.

In the denomination in which I serve, ordained elders have a right to a pastoral appointment to a local church. Because of the church's polity, it is tempting for pastors to see themselves as dependent upon the denominational structures. They see the denominational structures as an escalator that will eventually carry them to larger places of service. When this does not happen, they see the system as having failed them. Thus the denomination, not Jesus, becomes their Messiah. Thereby these pastors become what Jesus called "hired hands" instead of "shepherds" (John 10:12).

If we have allowed someone other than Jesus to be our Messiah, or if we have assumed the role of Messiah for someone else, it is time to change our minds. No one, no matter how wonderful he or she is, deserves to take Jesus' place in our life. And the worst thing about the disorder of codependency is that it is progressively compulsive. Codependents tend to become more and more obsessed. One person asks for more and more, and the other person is less and less able to say no. The only reason codependent people survive the pain is that they develop high pain thresholds.

Six Ways to Avoid Codependent Friendships

Here are six foolproof ways to avoid codependent friendships.

1.   Get It Clearly in Your Mind That You Are Not the Messiah

Early in John's gospel, the religious leaders asked John the Baptist, "Who are you?" His response was simple and profound: "I am not the Messiah" (John 1:19–20). He later repeated virtually the same words (John 3:28). John's answer was to tell people who he was not. I believe that until we have come to terms with not being the Messiah, we will never know who we are.

There is a needlepoint sign in the receiving area outside my office that reads, "There is a God—you're not Him!" Susan made it and gave it to me for Christmas many years ago. Some people think it is a put-down, but it is not. It is a liberating reminder to me not to take on the role of Messiah with people. I am not omniscient; I cannot know everything. I am not omnipresent; I cannot be there all the time. I am not omnipotent; I cannot do everything that needs to be done.

Get straight about it: You are not the Messiah.

2. Remember That Jesus Is the Messiah

Surrender yourself fully to Jesus. who said, "No one can serve two masters" (Matthew 6:24). There should be no divided loyalties in our lives. Neither other people nor damaged emotions should call the shots. Jesus, no one and nothing else, should be our Lord.

3. When Your Friends Have Burdens Too Big to Carry Alone, Help Them

Paul taught, "Bear one another's burdens and so fulfill the law of Christ" (Galatians 6:2). Or as the Golden Rule puts it, "In everything do to others as you would have them do to you" (Matthew 7:12).

Think of what it would be like for a group of us to go camping together. Let's say the campsite is several miles from where we park our cars, and there is a great deal of gear to carry in: Food, cooking equipment, tents, and such. We would not expect everyone to carry exactly the same weight, would we? Of course not. Everyone would be asked to carry the weight they were physically able to carry, and then those who were stronger would carry the additional weight. That is the way it should be with us relationally as well. Codependency occurs when we find ourselves carrying more than we should carry and allowing others to carry less than they are able to carry.

Do you know what it means to "spot" someone in weight lifting? It means you stand behind the bar and prevent the weighted bar from crushing the lifter. The object is to give the lifter as little assistance as possible. Ordinarily a spotter offers no more than a two-finger uplift on the bar, and only then if it is needed. Being a spotter is a good image for Christian people helping others.

4. When Your Burdens Are Too Great, Ask for Help

Rarely are friends called upon to be martyrs. Neither are we to pretend to be superhuman. None of us can carry all of life's crushing loads by ourselves. We all need help from time to time.

5. Expect Others to Carry Their Own Loads

"For all must carry their own load" (Galatians 6:5). The reverse of the Golden Rule is also true: We should refuse to do for others what they should do for themselves. If we carry the part of the load they need to carry, we weaken them.

What happens to the controller if the one who has been controlled starts providing for themselves? Pandemonium breaks loose.

What happens to the controlled person if the controller calls a halt to the rescuing habit? People throw fits.

Several years ago, I got a letter from a man I did not know who said he was desperate. He included in the envelope a bank statement and all his bills—not photocopies but originals. He said that he was surrendering his life to me and that whatever happened to him from now on was my responsibility. I called him immediately. Boy, was he mad when I told him that I would not be helping him. He called me every possible vulgar name—including a "hypocrite."

When we refuse to rescue people, they will resist. They will make us feel we are abandoning them. They will express fear and anger. They will act pitiful and try to make us feel guilty. They may even threaten to kill themselves. But we can remain healthy and have courage to set them free from the shackles of dependent behavior. George Youngblood, a teen addiction specialist, coined the phrase "Enabling is disabling." He is right.

6. We Must Carry Our Own Loads

No one else is responsible for your life, including your self-care. Other people are important, but so are we. Jesus' teaching to "love your neighbor as yourself" implies healthy self-regard (Matthew 22:39). How can you "love God as yourself" if you do not love yourself?

Reinhold Niebuhr wrote a prayer that is used widely in the Twelve Step community. It is called the Serenity Prayer. The words of this prayer provide us with guidelines for living interdependently: "God, grant me the serenity to accept the things I cannot change, the courage to change the things I can, and the wisdom to know the difference."

Several years ago, I saw a bumper sticker that read, "Let God Be God." I was offended by it at the time. Sometimes Christians put goofy things on their bumpers. What could "Let God Be God" mean? God is God. God does not require our permission to be God. But as the years passed, I have come to appreciate that message. I am not God, and you are not God. I am not the Messiah, and you are not the Messiah. We need to allow God to be God and Jesus to be the Messiah.

CHAPTER 8

A Fond Farewell?

"Some people are in your lives for a moment,
others for a season, and still others for a lifetime."

Unknown

The truth of this quotation is apparent, but like all forms of truth, it leaves us with as many questions as it does clarity. Are brief encounters meaningful? Why are so many meaningful relationships seasonal? What part should we play in ending relationships?

Just because people are in our lives temporarily, it does not mean relationships are not meaningful or transformational. Sometimes we hear a person speak, or we meet or know them briefly, and the relationship is life changing. I was around the missionary E. Stanley Jones for about an hour when I was in seminary. I never even shook his hand. Yet ever since then, he has been one of my heroes.

People can mean a great deal to us even when they are in our lives only for a season. These friendships, interrupted by circumstances, unresolved conflict, or death, nonetheless can play an instrumental role in our lives. On my first day in seminary, a British theological professor showed up at our apartment door. He stayed for supper and led us in the evening prayer from the Anglican Book of Common Prayer. For the next few years, that professor had a huge shaping influence in my life. We regularly shared our lives together. His influence is still with me.

And praise God, there are a few people who are permanent parts of our lives. These are our "until death do us part" covenant friends.

The movie *Shall We Dance?* was a romantic comedy about John Clark, a successful Chicago estate planning attorney with a beautiful wife and two lovely teenage daughters. He had everything going for him. Nevertheless; he sensed something was missing in his life. One evening on the train ride to his suburban home, John caught a glimpse of a beautiful woman looking out the window of a dance studio. Suddenly he knew what was missing. His well-ordered, predictable life needed the freedom and spark of the dance floor. Soon John started coming home later from work. And his excuses didn't make sense. John's wife, Beverly, grew suspicious that he was having an affair. She hired a private detective to track him. The detective reported that John was not in love with another woman. His new love was dancing. In the verbal interchange with the detective, Beverly shared a piercing insight: Covenant people in our lives are our permanent witnesses. These are the ones who know the most about us, who witness our lives. Unfortunately, there are far too few people in this category.

Many times, relationships pass through our lives or come to an end due to no fault of our own or of the other person. But there are other times when things happen that cause friendships to come to an unfortunate and untimely end.

Things That Destroy Friendships

There are at least six reasons why friendships fizzle out.

1) Marriage

Marriage can actually cause existing friendships to die. Married couples are usually attracted to different types of friends. The attraction of one spouse to a friend is no guarantee that the other spouse will like that person. Four-way couple friendships that predate the marriage are scarce. Marriage is far more likely to weaken the fabric of existing friendships than it is to strengthen them. The reasons for this loss are varied, such as jealousy, habits, new obligations, and differences in tastes. When people get married, former friends ordinarily have to find time for each other during non-family hours, or the relationship will eventually become past tense.

2) Divorce

Marital divorce ends many friendships. When people go through divorce, it strains their couple friendships. The question is, "Which one is going to be our friend?" It is easier to opt not to choose sides and to drop them both, especially once they enter the dating world. People who have gone through divorce almost universally report that there is something about divorce that feels threatening to married folks. It probably reminds them that their marriage may not be safe—that divorce could uncouple them as well. People going through divorce also consistently express the feeling that they are "half a couple." Strained friendships go with divorce.

3) Death

Death ends friendships. I have participated in a men's forum group for more than twenty years. Several years ago, we were projecting how many years we might have left to live. I asked a question: "If I could guarantee you that you could live to be eighty-five, remaining in reasonably good health, and then dropping dead, would you sign on?" Every member of the group but one said they would agree to a deal like that. One group member said, "No, I would want more time than that." Sadly, he was dead within two years, far in advance of his eighty-fifth year, and it broke our hearts. We all have far too few real friends, and when one dies, the loss is overwhelming.

4) Ethical Violations

Ann Hibhard had it right when she wrote, "Disappointment is inevitable for one reason: We can only have sinners for friends."[1] Sometimes relationships end because friends prove to be unethical. They show themselves to be liars, thieves, backstabbers, adulterers, deceivers, or abusers. Trust is broken. And friendship ends.

5) Betrayal

Our friends are in a privileged position in our lives. Therefore, when our friends betray us, it can destroy the friendship. The Apocrypha suggests that the betrayer should seize the initiative in terminating the relationship: "Whoever betrays secrets destroys confidence, and never finds a congenial friend. Love your friend and keep faith with him; but if you betray his secrets, do not follow after him. For as a person destroys his enemy, so you have destroyed the friendship of your neighbor" (Sirach 27:16–18).

Jesus was betrayed by one of his closest friends. He chose Judas not just as an apostle, but also as the group's treasurer (Mark 3:13–19; John 12:6). He trusted Judas. Even though Jesus knew Judas would betray him, he gave him a final chance to alter his course. Jesus washed Judas' feet and shared the Last Supper with him (John 13:5). Later that night, when Judas came with the temple guards for the arrest, Jesus still called him "friend" (Matthew 26:50). Imagine the pain Judas' betrayal caused Jesus.

Betrayal is far too common among friends. Sometimes we justify betrayal as meaningless loose talk. Blaise Pascal noted, "Few friendships would endure if each knew what his friend said of him in his absence."[2] One television series coined a word for friends who betray trust: Frenemy. Frenemies are friends who behave as enemies.

6) Drifting Apart

Sometimes friendships unravel gradually because the people involved drift apart. Soon the relationship is on life support, and both parties are wondering if it is not time to pull the plug. Nothing in life is static, especially relationships. Here are six examples of things that cause friendships to drift apart:

A. Neglect. Sometimes the drift is caused by benign neglect. Sometimes we need different friends at different seasons of our lives. We are evolving, and so is our friend. Gradually we become attracted to different people. Because we do not nurture the relationship, what follows is distance, indifference, and death. Like an unnourished plant, friendships can wither, decay, and die.

B. Selfishness. Sometimes selfishness is the culprit. We do not invest in the relationship because there is no longer any gain in it for us. The more we see friendship in a utilitarian way, the easier it is to end it. In other words, the more we see a friendship as something that benefits us, the more likely we will be to end it when it no longer benefits us. There is no reason left to associate, so we trade up. The friendship drifts apart because it was counterfeit from the beginning.

C. Loss of common interests. Sometimes the activities that once cemented the relationship no longer hold. When this glue is gone, the relationship no longer seems valuable. The friendship is therefore prioritized downward. Sociologists call this "differential growth." These changes take place for numerous reasons. For example, involvement in Twelve Step groups usually brings about a change in interests and an exposure to a new community of friends.

D. Change in location. Moving sometimes lessens the opportunities for us to be with friends. If we are not intentional about maintaining communication, the relationship is dwarfed. Important things happen in the lives of our friends without our awareness. Because of the means of instant, effective communication at our disposal, the activity of friendships need not be terminated because of relocation. Nevertheless, absence rarely makes the heart grow fonder.

E. Relational time-outs. Sometimes it makes sense to take a break in the relationship. There are things we need to do, changes we need to make, and our friend is not supportive. So for a while, the relationship is strained—we have little contact. Later, we miss our friend, and the relationship is patched up. Other times, the breach is never mended.

F. Unresolved conflict. Sometimes quarrels become enmity, and people who were once friends become enemies. Unfortunately, there are times when the conflicts are unresolvable, when amends are impossible. It is even more common for friction to cause friends to withdraw without an explanation, making reconciliation impossible. There are even times when people manufacture a conflict to exit the relationship, when the conflict is merely an excuse for terminating the friendship.

Images of Friendship Termination

Four unthinkable images come to mind about terminating covenant friendships.

1) Sacraments

The first image involves the two main sacraments of the church: Baptism and Holy Communion. These sacraments are everyday reminders of how we are covenantally connected to God. Baptism symbolizes that we belong to Christ and one another through the Lord Jesus. There is "one Lord, one faith, one baptism" (Ephesians 4:5). Holy Communion likewise symbolizes our union with Christ and Christian community. We are "one body . . . one loaf" (1 Corinthians 10:17).

Friendship is sacramental because it portrays how "God's grace flows from one person to another."3 Friendship is holy because it is how God's love is revealed to us in community. As we love one another, we experience being loved by God. As Carmon L. Caltagirone puts it, "God reveals himself through the real life presence of those around us."4

So then, what does it mean to terminate a covenant friendship? Is it not like nullifying a baptism or denying someone Holy Communion? Breaking off a covenant friendship is a radical step.

2) Trinity

A second image relates to the Trinity. Throughout Christian history, it has been common for theologians to compare Christian friendship and the holy Trinity. Here is how the analogy goes: The relationship of the three persons of the Trinity form the perfect model for friendship. The Trinity is not three disjointed entities operating in isolation but a community of shared divine intimacy. Rather than competing with one another, the three holy Persons defer to one another in love.

In a similar way, our covenant friends are the other halves of us. They are our alter egos. Even though our friends are not like us, they are coequal with us. When we operate in unity, we make up a whole person. When friendship is at its best, we defer to one another in love rather than competing with one another.

What would it mean, then, for a covenant friendship to be terminated? Is that not like a fracture in the holy Trinity? Breaking off a covenant friendship is a radical step.

3) Marriage

A third image that demonstrates how serious it is to end a covenant friendship is divorce. As we talked about in Chapter 3: The Beauty of Covenant Friendship, marriage is not contractual; it is a covenantal relationship. Covenants are not intended to be terminated. When people make a covenant, they are bonded; "the two become one flesh" (Genesis 2:24).

Divorce is one person saying to the other person with whom they are bonded, "I am hereby breaking the covenant I entered into when we got married. I don't want you anymore!" Divorce is like tearing apart something that had once been inseparable. People going through divorce describe feeling as if someone ripped off a body part without benefit of anesthesia.

Jesus said divorce occurs because people's hearts get hard (Matthew 19:8). Human frailties and constant friction over time cause our hearts to get hard, and we take the fragments of our broken dreams up the courthouse steps—something we once thought unimaginable.

If covenant friends are bonded into oneness, is not the ending of the friendship like divorce—the dissolving of an indissoluble union? Breaking off a covenant friendship is a radical step.

4) Adoption

Another covenant mentioned in chapter 3 was adoption. When families adopt a child, they become permanently united to him or her. In the ancient world, children who were adopted could not be disowned, but natural children could.

What, then, does it mean to terminate a covenant friendship? Is it not like disowning an adopted child? Breaking off a covenant friendship is a radical step.

Friendship Divorce

Remember the covenant friendship between Barnabas and Paul? Time and time again, Barnabas stood by and encouraged Paul. He was Paul's mentor. Barnabas was the team leader of their first missionary trip. His name was usually mentioned prior to Paul's in the Acts narrative (Acts 13:2, 7; 14:12, 14; 15:12). The one-two punch of this dynamic duo made them a fruitful missionary team.

Acts 15:36–41 describes the death of their friendship. On their first mission venture, Barnabas and Paul had taken a young tagalong named John Mark. John Mark was a cousin of Barnabas (Colossians 4:10). Halfway through the trip, John Mark got homesick and returned to his mama.

As Barnabas and Paul prepared for their second mission trip, Barnabas renominated John Mark as an assistant. Paul's pent-up frustrations with John Mark erupted, and he vetoed the idea. A "sharp disagreement" broke out between them (Acts 15:39). Barnabas, ever the encourager, wanted to give John Mark a second chance. Paul saw the decision as a matter of principle. He thought taking an immature person on the second missionary journey was too risky. The issue became heated, so the two men parted company. Barnabas took John Mark, and they returned to Cyprus. Paul chose Silas as his new partner, and they went to Syria, Cilicia, and ultimately to Europe. As far as we know, the two men never reconciled. They could not find a way to put Humpty Dumpty together again. Their friendship divorce was final.

How to Restore a Damaged Friendship

There is an old verse that speaks about relationships "To live above with the saints we love, ah, that will be pure glory. But to live below with the saints we know, ah, that's another story."

Relationships are difficult. Conflicts are inevitable, even

between close friends. Through the years, 90 percent of the pastoral problems people have brought to me were about relational issues. Chances are that each of us has been in a relational hole we found hard to climb out of.

We have too few covenant friendships, and we cannot afford to lose any of them. True friendships are not disposable or easily replaceable. So let's learn how to fix them—to love instead of leave. Here are some steps we can take to improve the chances of reconciliation.

Be Open to Your Blind Spots

First, be open to your own blind spots. Most of us have lost a close friend or two along the way. And chances are that it was for one of the same reasons that destroyed the friendship of Barnabas and Paul: Unrecognized blind spots. All of us have blind spots, but few of us recognize them.

Sometimes family is a blind spot. Barnabas was committed to the spiritual formation of his cousin. His philosophy was, "Love me, love John Mark." For Paul, the decision about who to take on the missionary journey was strictly about the bottom line: Which persons can help us drive the mission to its desired results. There is no indication that the two men recognized or discussed the blind spots that stood between them.

A second blind spot was the difference in their temperaments. Barnabas, on one hand, was a kind and sensitive man. He was gentle, gracious, and generous. He was nonjudgmental, compassionate, and tolerant. Barnabas was an encourager. Paul, on the other hand, was strident and confrontational by nature (Galatians 2:11). He was uncompromising and unbending, more interested in achieving the goal than in sparing people's feelings. Paul saw everything as being black or white. And when he made up his mind about a matter, there was little chance of changing it.

A physician friend used to say there were two kinds of folks: control freaks and escape artists. If that's so, Paul was the control freak and Barnabas was the escape artist. Paul's nature was to stand, fight, and never surrender. Barnabas was more likely to withdraw from conflict. Were Paul and Barnabas aware that the difference in their temperaments was one of the causes of their division? Did they discuss these differences? We are not told.

A third blind spot in the two men was their priorities. For Barnabas, priority one was people. He had a micro vision of ministry. He refused to see someone he loved thrown under the bus. After all, did not Paul write, "Love bears all things, believes all things, hopes all things, endures all things. Love never ends." (1 Corinthians 13:7–8)? Barnabas saw the same long-term possibilities in John Mark that he had seen in Paul. Why shouldn't John Mark be given the same kind of second chance Barnabas had extended to Paul?

Paul had a macro-vision of ministry, and John Mark had proved to be a deserter. He was guilty of dereliction of duty. There was no reason to trust a person who had proved to be untrustworthy in the past. The stakes were too high. Both men had a legitimate point of view. They were both right—from their perspectives. Were the two men aware that they saw truth from different starting points? Did they ever discuss these differences? We are not sure.

A fourth blind spot was the difference in the spiritual gifts of the two men. Barnabas had pastoral gifts. He was interested in nurturing John Mark so that he continued to grow as a disciple of Jesus. Paul was a prophet, a spare-no-one's-feelings truth-teller. He was also a missionary-evangelist, always eager to break new mission ground, never willing to go where the church had already been established (Acts 15:20).

Usually the sources of our conflict with people exist internally before they ever manifest externally. Our personal internal battles have a way of spilling over into our relationships. Do you see this principle in the conflict between Barnabas and Paul? The real source of their conflict was rooted in who they were and how they saw reality. Both men were so committed to their worldview that they stopped being able to communicate respectfully with the other person.

Usually when the real source of the conflict is internal differences, we are unaware of it. We can't see that we are looking at the same thing from two different perspectives. So the intensity of our conversation ratchets up, the communication misfires, an emotional volcano erupts, and the only apparent choice is to part company. Friendship is dismantled. Unfortunately, this kind of high-minded relational dismantling happens often between good and godly people.

Can you see how some of these same inner commitments have affected your former relationships? Before you make any attempt to reconcile with a friend, take a long look at yourself. Ask the Holy Spirit to turn a spotlight on your soul and expose the hidden things inside you that are causing part of the relational difficulty. Then ask the Spirit to give you revelation about your friend's internal issues.

Understand the Difference between Forgiveness and Reconciliation

Second, understand the difference between forgiveness and reconciliation. Some people throw away their friendships easily. Their friend does something displeasing to them, so they rip him or her out of their lives. Isn't it strange how we forget all that our friend has done for us in the past when conflict arises? Grace from previous efforts evaporates. All we care about is the issue at hand. Forgiveness and reconciliation, which are the heart of the gospel, are therefore impossible.

We need both forgiveness and reconciliation, but first we need to learn the difference between the two.

Forgiveness has nothing to do with the other person. Forgiveness is strictly about our relationship with God. That is why King David said to God, "Against you, you alone have I sinned, and done what is evil in your sight" (Psalm 51:4). He said the only person he had sinned against was God. But had he not committed adultery and murder? Didn't those sins involve other people? Why, then, does David make this confusing statement? It's because forgiveness and reconciliation are two different things. Forgiveness is about our relationship with God. Reconciliation is about our relationship with others.

Jesus points out this principle in his teaching on prayer. He said that if we are not willing to forgive others, God would not forgive us (Matthew 5:12, 14–15). Unwillingness to forgive destroys the bridge over which forgiveness comes to us. The Lord's Prayer references forgiveness, not reconciliation.

To forgive is to surrender the right to get even, to release the other person from our emotional clutches, and to turn the whole matter over to God. Jesus said in the parable of the unforgiving servant that if we do not forgive, we get turned over to the "torturers" (Matthew 18:23–35). And guess where the torturers live? Inside us!

Forgiveness is hard, especially when a friend has offended us. It is easier to forgive an enemy than a friend, because the wounds of a friend carry the extra pain of disappointment.

What are we to do when someone offends us? As the Lord's Prayer says, we are to pray, "Lord, forgive me as I forgive _____" (Matthew 6:12,14–15). Fill in the blank with that person's name. Who is it? It is the most important person in your life, because it is the person who is preventing you from receiving the forgiveness of God!

Our forgiveness of others can take place in a flash. When we turn the offense over to God and surrender the right to get even, we are forgiven. But what happens if there is a repeat of the infraction by the same person, so the next time we pray, we have to put the same person's name in the blank again? It is simple: We repeat the process of forgiveness. Jesus said our forgiveness of others is to be as unconditional as God's forgiveness of us (Matthew 18:21–22).

When we have wronged others, forgiveness is harder. It requires us to do two things: Face our error honestly (Matthew 7:3–5) and make amends (Luke 19:8), unless making amends makes matters worse. Sometimes acknowledging errors to the offended party and making restitution does more harm than good. We each must weigh this honestly for ourselves.

No friendship can endure long without forgiveness. Proverbs 17:9 says, "One who forgives an affront fosters friendship, but one who dwells on disputes will alienate a friend." A friend of mine likes to quote the old adage that says, "A real friend is one who, when you have made a mistake, doesn't think you have done a permanent job of it."

The assumption among covenant friends should be that offenses will be forgiven. When this is the case, it makes fair-minded debate and strong disagreement possible. Friends can collide verbally with no fear of reprisals or being regarded as enemies. Friends begin difficult conversations with the assurance that, regardless of what is said, love and forgiveness will prevail. As the Bible says repeatedly, "Love covers a multitude of sins" (Proverbs 10:12; James 5:20; 1 Peter 4:8).

Let this be clear: Receiving God's forgiveness does not mean we are reconciled to the other person. It means we are reconciled to God. Forgiveness and reconciliation are fundamentally different. There is no reason to believe Barnabas and Paul did not forgive one another. But there is ample evidence that there was no reconciliation. The two issues are different. Forgiveness is vertical; it is between us and God. Reconciliation is horizontal; it is between our friends and us. Forgiveness can happen in a moment. Reconciliation is a relational process and sometimes a very long process.

The Reconciliation Process

The process of reconciliation means that the friendship is back at square one and the division has been healed. God aches for us to be reconciled and for our broken relationships to be healed (Matthew 5:23–26). Each of us is to pursue reconciliation (Matthew 5:9; 2 Corinthians 5:20; 1 Peter 3:11), but it is a two-way street. It requires patient cooperation and the rebuilding of trust. We cannot unilaterally force reconciliation. Unfortunately, some of our broken relationships will not be repaired on this side of the border of life. Ultimately, heaven is our last shot at reconciliation.

Laura Davis points out that we would be better off seeing reconciliation as a continuum rather than an all-or-nothing transaction. She suggests we should think of four different levels of reconciliation:

Levels of Reconciliation

- Level One: No relationship is possible at this time.
- Level Two: The relationship is cordial, but there is minimal contact.
- Level Three: One person unilaterally alters his/her perceptions, expectations, and boundaries regarding the relationship, even though the other person does not reciprocate.
- Level Four: Intimacy is restored for both parties. It is as if the troubling incident had never happened.[5]

Sometimes we try to make reconciliation happen prematurely, but our feeble attempts don't deal with the real issues. David and his oldest son, Absalom, had a superficial healing of their relationship (2 Samuel 14:25–33). Things looked as if they were back to normal on the surface, but nothing was ever resolved. Soon after the window-dressing reconciliation, Absalom fomented a revolt against his dad, usurping his father's throne (2 Samuel 15).

Relational intimacy cannot take place when the chief aim of both parties is conflict avoidance. When the rule is, "Do not say or do anything that will rock the boat or increase the conflict," true feelings and concerns have to be withheld. However well-intended conflict avoidance might be, it is misguided. Our goal should be conflict resolution, not conflict avoidance. Conflict resolution involves confronting the real issues and staying faithful to a reconciliation process.

We should wholeheartedly seek to restore injured friendships. Paul wrote, "If it is possible, so far as it depends on you, live peaceably with all" (Romans 12:18).

Here are five steps that can lead to reconciliation:

1. Negotiate the Time and Place for a Peace Conference
Do not triangulate. Talking to a third party about the issues is more likely to create a wall of misunderstanding than it is to provide solutions (Matthew 18:15). The person you talk to, because they are hearing only your side of the story, is not likely to help with reconciliation. They have a jaundiced view of what happened. Triangulation may increase your feeling of self-justification for one party, but it will ultimately decrease the likelihood of reconciliation.

2. Ask God to Help You Discern the Real Causes of the Conflict
There is an Asian proverb that says, "In order to untie a knot, you must first understand how it was tied." Here are some questions to meditate on as you try to gain this understanding:

- What went wrong?
- In what way was I at fault?
- In what way was the other person at fault?
- How does the other person view the situation? In what way is he/she correct?
- How much of the problem has to do with internal differences between us?
- What are the other person's terms of reconciliation?
- Is it possible to remove this person from my inner circle of friends but keep them in a larger circle of friendship until the relationship is restored?
- What are some positive solutions to the crisis?

3. Express a Desire for Reconciliation

See if the two of you can agree on some basic ground rules for discussion. For example, take turns talking and listening for ten minutes each. When you talk . . .

- Affirm the importance of the relationship
- Confess your faults (James 5:16); do not let pride hold you back
- Use "I" statements instead of "you" statements
- Use "I feel" statements instead of "I think" statements
- Stick to the subject at hand; do not discuss past issues
- Make sure all the words you speak are kind (Proverbs 12:18; Ephesians 4:29)
- Do not raise your voice (Proverbs 15:1)
- If you ask for changes, ask for behavioral changes, not thought or feeling alterations
- Express your willingness to start over
- Again, affirm the value of the relationship

When you listen . . .

- Give your full attention to what is being said, and make sure your body language communicates this as well
- Watch for your friend's nonverbal communication
- Do not interrupt
- When they finish talking, summarize what you heard, ask if you heard them correctly, and ask questions for further clarification

4. Look for Win-Win Solutions

If the conversation goes well, brainstorm possible win-win solutions. A win-win solution means cooperation in which both people win.

- Competition—"I win, you lose"
- Capitulation—"You win, I lose"
- Compromise—"We both lose"
- Cooperation—"We both win"

If there is a solution both parties can reach consensus on, give it a try. Agree on what each of you is going to do and when you will meet again to discuss your progress. Thank the other person for agreeing to meet, for their candid discussion, for their efforts to negotiate a solution, and for agreeing to meet again in the future.

5. Third-Party Mediation

If none of the above strategies work, see if the two of you can agree on one to three unbiased, third-party mediators (Matthew 18:16–17). This mediator or mediators will function as "peacemaker" (Matthew 5:9). It would be good if both parties could agree in advance to abide by the outcome of the mediation. It has been my experience that non-legal but ethically binding mediation is a very effective way to resolve disputes.

Occasionally, time heals old wounds—not often, but occasionally. We change, the other person changes, and in time, both parties see things differently. It is time for the rest of the story about Barnabas, Paul, and John Mark. Paul's letters give an indication that the relationship between Paul and John Mark is finally healed. In his final epistle, Paul writes to Timothy and asks him, "Get Mark and bring him with you, for he is useful in my ministry" (2 Timothy 4:11). The fellow who broke up the partnership of Barnabas and Paul was now thought to be "useful." Something changed, probably in both Paul and John Mark. Later Mark also partnered with Peter (1 Peter 5:13), and the result was Mark's gospel. Mark even wrote himself into the story. He was the young man in the Gethsemane account who became the first "streaker" (Mark 14:51–52).

Terminating Friendships

Third, unfortunately, not all friendships are reconcilable. The church father Jerome said, "Friendship which can end was never true friendship."[8] I beg to differ. The grim reality is that some friendships do come to an end (Matthew 10:14, 34-37; 18:17; Luke 9:59-62; 1 Corinthians 5:4–13; 2 Corinthians 2:6–8; Titus 3:10–11). Sometimes our friends are on an entirely different trajectory, and there is no way for us to come together again.

My own experience with ending relationships has been difficult. Nothing I have ever dealt with has been so painful. No one teaches us how to end friendships well.

In the time of Jesus, the Hebrew people had a ritual for ending relationships. It was called kazazah.[9] When a relationship was being terminated, the person ending the relationship would break an earthen vessel in the presence of the offender and witnesses, symbolically saying, "You are cut off from me." No doubt the prodigal in Jesus' parable expected a kazazah ceremony when he asked for his inheritance prior to his father's death (Luke 15:12).

Does divorcing friends sound un-Christian? After all, isn't God's love unconditional and unlimited? (Exodus 34:6–7). Maybe so, but we are not God. There comes a time when the healthiest thing we can do is to cut the cord and move on. Moving on involves drawing new boundaries, grieving the loss, learning the lessons the relationship taught, and hoping for future reconciliation in this world or the next.

It is a radical thing to shift what we thought was a lifetime friendship to the seasonal variety. Terminating covenant friendships takes an emotional toll on us. It is not like "defriending" someone on Facebook. There are feelings of loss and melancholy that go with ending any relationship, much less a covenant friendship. It is the death of our other self. It is like having a loved one die when their corpse is still walking around. When a covenant friendship ends, take the time to grieve the loss and assimilate the lessons the relationship taught you.

It is also important to undergo some sort of ritual by which the bond is broken—something similar to the Jewish kazazah ceremony. As you consider what elements to put in the ritual, this prayer by Joyce Rupp is worth considering:

God of beginnings and endings, grant that I might have the strength to put an end to this matter which has weighed so heavily on my heart and my mind. Grant that I might bid farewell to this relationship which has brought me so much pain and grief. Know that this dying which is so evident in the process of termination will truly be a step into new life for me. I feel fragile and frail at this moment, even though I know it is the right direction and decision for me. Help me to close the door on this section of my journey, to walk into new rooms of life. I need to experience a freshness and a vitality like the cool breeze of a spring morning coming through an open window. Be this vitality for me, God of compassion. Grant that I may turn my back and walk away from what has been. I pray that I may be healed of this hurt, and I pray that any whom I have hurt through this experience may also be healed. Amen.[10]

CHAPTER 9

You've Got a Friend

"I cannot imagine a genuine human friendship where true love flourishes that is not grounded in a shared dream of the kingdom."

Carmen Caltagirone

The memory of a middle-aged man's words still burns in my mind. He was part of a seminary group to which I had been assigned. None of us really wanted to participate in these small-group sessions. The group leader guided us into a discussion about loneliness and the need for friendship. My colleague, who had not spoken a dozen words the entire term, suddenly blurted out, "I'm desperately lonely! I'm so lonely I could die! If I don't find a friend soon, it is going to kill me! I'd take a dog!" I froze in horror, not knowing what to say or do.

I have wondered what happened to that fellow through the years. And each time I thought about him, I wondered how many people like him surround me. I have a suspicion that he was not unique. He was just more candid than most people. The craving for intimacy is universal. None of us can survive as loners (Genesis 2:18).

One of the defining characteristics of Jesus' three-year ministry was the priority he placed on friendship. Notice two amazing things about Jesus' relational world.

Jesus: The Model for Friendship

If you want to learn about friendship, let Jesus be your model. I grew up singing a gospel song called "What a Friend We Have in Jesus."[1] If I were a poet, I would write a song about Jesus' friendship model: "What a Friendship Model We Have in Jesus." Jesus is the perfect example of the kinds of friends we should aim at having and being. He had four distinct types of friends.

1. Casual Friends

Jesus loved the world and everybody in it (John 3:16). He cared about the multitude (Mark 4:1)—people we would call acquaintances. Jesus saw humanity as sheep, and he thought of himself as their shepherd (Mark 6:34). Jesus taught them (Mark 4:1–2), fed them (Mark 6:35–44; 8:1–9), and healed them (Mark 1:32–34). He regarded each of them as pre-disciples, those who might choose at any time to align themselves with his highest priority, God's kingdom (Mark 4:2–32). In this sense, Jesus' friendships were not exclusive.

The multitude included people who were hostile to Jesus and aspired to kill him. For example, he healed the daughter of Jairus, a synagogue leader in Galilee, even though Jairus may well have already conspired to kill him (Mark 3:6; 5:21–24, 35–42). Jesus treated everyone he encountered in a loving way, and we need to do the same. We are to love our neighbors as ourselves (Leviticus 19:19:18; Mark 12:31).

None of us can have an enduring, intimate relationship with everyone. Though Jesus was kind to Jairus' daughter, we have no reason to believe that he had an ongoing relationship with Jairus. An English proverb makes the same point: "A friend of all is a friend of none."[2]

2. Disciple Friends

Jesus had people who followed him and learned from him. They were disciples—a term that means "followers, learners." Jesus considered his disciples as friends (John 15:13–15) and family (Mark 3:31–35). Jesus and his disciple friends had shared kingdom values. As the adage goes, "Birds of a feather flock together." Many of Jesus' disciples were women who funded his ministry (Luke 8:1–3). We know of at least one occasion when this band of people included seventy people. Jesus sent them out to do good on his behalf (Luke 10: 1–20).

Oddly enough, Jesus' biological family members were not his disciple friends during his lifetime (Mark 3:31–35; John 7:5). They showed a lack of understanding and often open hostility toward his ministry (Mark 3:20–21). On the cross, Jesus delegated responsibility for his mother to the apostle John, even though he had siblings (John 19:26–27; Mark 6:3). It was only after Jesus' death and resurrection that Jesus' brother James became the leader of the Jerusalem church (Mark 6:3; Acts 1:4,14; 2:1; 15:13; 1 Corinthians 15:7).

In a similar way, the apostles regarded their followers as friends. Paul calls Philemon a "dear friend" (Philemon 1). The apostle John urged his readers "Greet the friends by name" (3 John 15). It is for this reason that the Quakers refer to themselves as Friends.

The first place to look for friends is within the community of faith. In order to find and cultivate friends in a church family, we must do more than attend worship. We need to take advantage of face-to-face opportunities, like small groups and service projects.

Must there be emotional and theological similarity in these disciple friendships? Not necessarily. Our believing friends can differ broadly from us. There are two common denominators necessary for disciple friendship to flourish. First, we each need to make God's kingdom priority one (Matthew 6:33; 1 Corinthians 15:33; 2 Corinthians 6:14). Carmen Caltagirone makes this point clearly: "I cannot imagine a genuine human friendship where true love flourishes that is not grounded in a shared dream of the Kingdom."[3] And second, we need to love one another (John 13:34–35; 15:12; 1 John 4:7–12). When we disagree, we need to be agreeable about it. We need to agree to disagree and resolve to love one another.

Does that mean friendship with non-Christians is ruled out? No, not if these people meet these two criteria: seeking kingdom values and having the capacity to love. I have seen these qualities in Jews, Muslims, Buddhists, Hindus, Sikhs, atheists, and all manner of other humans.

3. Close Friends

Jesus chose twelve people from the larger group of disciples to be his close covenant friends. Most people can manage far fewer covenant friendships. David and Ruth each had only one. Jesus had a larger covenant friendship band than most of us can support.

Jesus called these special friends to do two things: to stay close to him and to do the things he was doing (Mark 3:13–19). Jesus lived his life in community with the twelve. He walked with them, talked with them, ate with them, slept with them, and ministered with them.

If Jesus needed close friends, how much more do we need them? There is a group of believers in a city in Georgia who demonstrate this kind of kingdom closeness to me. They call themselves "the Gang." These couples have been intentional about their friendship for many years. They are members of different churches. They have different economic means. These differences do not seem to matter to them. What counts are their love for God's kingdom and their love for each other. They eat together regularly, travel together periodically, pray for each other daily, and stand by each other loyally. It is a friendship network in which each feels closer than siblings. Even though I have not lived in Columbus for many years, I am blessed to be counted in their number.

Tragically, Jesus' closest friends failed him. He asked them to watch and pray with him in the garden of Gethsemane. They had promised to stay close to him and to do what he did, but instead of watching and praying, they fell asleep time and time again (Mark 14:32–42). Two of Jesus' closest friends turned on him—they betrayed and denied knowing him (Mark 14:10–11, 17–21, 66–72).

4. Intimate Friends

In addition to his twelve apostles, Jesus had an even closer inner circle of friends. Most of the time it included only Peter, James, and John (Mark 5:37; 9:2; 14:33), but occasionally Andrew was included (Mark 13:3). With these intimates, Jesus withheld nothing. In the Gospel that bears his name, John claimed to be the closest of Jesus' intimate friends. John referred to himself as "the disciple whom he loved" (John 13:23; 19:26; 21:7, 20). He sat in a position of honor, next to Jesus, at the Last Supper (John 13:23). John was the only apostle present when Jesus was dying on the cross (John 19:25–27). Jesus asked John to care for his mother after his death (John 19:27).

There is a compelling story in Mark 2:1–12 about a paralyzed man brought on a pallet to Jesus by four friends. When the crowd in the house was too large to get him through the door, the four friends uncovered the roofing of the house and lowered their buddy into Jesus' presence. Imagine the homeowner's shock as he felt straw fall on his head and then saw the sun or moon shining into his house. The four friends refused to allow any barrier to stand in the way of their friend's healing. Jesus saw their action as an expression of faith (Mark 2:5). We all need four intimate friends who would not allow any obstacle to prevent them from helping us.

We cannot be equally close, even with our closest friends. There should be a few people, probably no more than four, from whom we withhold nothing. These intimate friends should know everything there is to know about us.

Each of us needs to be intentional about having at least these three categories of friends: disciple friends, close friends, and intimate friends.

Jesus: The Means of Friendship

In the fifteenth chapter of John's gospel, Jesus gave an extended discourse on friendship. Jesus stated that our first relational priority should be with him, and loyalty to other friends should be second.

Jesus said he takes first priority because we draw our life from him. He offers an example from horticulture to explain what he meant. Jesus says he is like a vine, and we are like branches on the vine. Our inner lives come from union with Christ, not from ourselves or one another (John 15:1–8). When we draw life from ourselves, we run dry. When we draw life from one another, our relationships become codependent.

Reflect on Jesus' exact words about our union with him: "Abide in me as I abide in you. Just as the branch cannot bear fruit by itself unless it abides in the vine, neither can you unless you abide in me. I am the vine, you are the branches. Those who abide in me and I in them bear much fruit, because apart from me you can do nothing" (John 15:4–5).

Here is my paraphrase of these words: "Remain intentionally connected to me. Find your life in me. Live dependent on me. Stay attached to me at all times. Let my relationship with you have priority and privilege in your life. Be aware that I am living in you. Just as a branch cannot bear fruit independent of the vine—it must stay connected, so you are not able to be spiritually fruitful all by yourself. Apart from connectedness to me you can do nothing permanent and nothing that ultimately makes any difference."

Paul's letters support the notion that we are in a mystical union with the risen Christ. We are to see ourselves as "in Christ" so that when God looks at us, he sees his Son covering us (2 Corinthians 5:17). Spiritual growth does not happen by trying to get closer to Christ through the practice of spiritual disciplines. Spiritual growth occurs when we embrace our existing union with Christ. We practice spiritual disciplines not to draw closer to Christ but because we are in him. Paul, who never knew the earthly Jesus (1 Corinthians 15:8), saw himself as being so spiritually united to Christ that he wrote, "I have been crucified with Christ; it is no longer I who live, but Christ who lives in me. And the life I now live in the flesh I live by faith in the Son of God, who loved me and gave himself for me" (Galatians 2:19–20).

It is easy to see how union with the Lord Jesus would transform our relationships with others who are also abiding in him. Our vertical friendship with Jesus enables and empowers horizontal friendships with other Christ followers.

On a recent trip to New York City, I discovered that a Second Avenue subway line was being built. This subway line will eventually connect to other parts of the city's vast underground system. Engineers and construction crews have been working on it for several years, and they project that it will take several more years to complete. In order to drill through the bedrock under the city, they use drills twelve times stronger than a 747 jet engine. The work is slow, and it takes place far below the surface of the earth.

The Holy Spirit does in us what those huge drills are doing to the solid rock underneath New York City. When we actively flesh out what it means to be the body of Christ, the Spirit pierces the hardness in our souls, helping us to connect transparently with

God and others. It is a slow and painful process, invisible to those who have casual relationships with us. They do not see the changes taking place because they occur in the hidden places of our hearts. We "are being transformed into Christ's image from one degree of glory to another . . . by the Spirit" (2 Corinthians 3:18). These inner alterations make it more and more possible for us to connect with other Christians in healthy ways. Our job is to collaborate with the Holy Spirit by risking transparency with safe people.

It can also be said that the quality of our friendship with Jesus determines the quality of our friendships with others. Covenant friendships are grounded in the life of the living Jesus that flows through us. Without this connectedness to Jesus, our friendships break down and become dysfunctional. Therefore, Jesus is the means by which we experience friendship.

Here are some examples from John's gospel of things our friend Jesus, does for us. These are also things we can do for our friends.

Praying for Our Friends

Jesus prayed for his disciples during his lifetime, and he prays for us now. One of Jesus' most remarkable prayers is recorded in John 17. There are two parts of the prayer: Jesus' prayer for his original twelve apostles (vv. 1–19) and his intercession for future disciples, including us (vv. 20–26). Jesus prayed two things for his future disciples: first, that we might be unified so that the world may believe that God sent Jesus into the world; and second, that we may be indwelt by the life and love of Jesus.

Paul tells us what Jesus is doing right now: He is at the right hand of God praying for us (Romans 8:34), and he is acting as our defense attorney with God (1 John 2:1–2). Both these images are about Jesus being our intercessor. When people understand that Jesus is praying for them, it is the most natural thing in the world for them to take the burdens of their friends to Jesus. I have often said that if we have a friend in need and we do not pray, it is either because we do not believe enough or we do not care enough. If we believe in the presence and power of Christ and care about our friends, should we not pray for them?

The prayers of Jesus are powerful. Jesus said to Peter, "Simon, Simon, Satan has demanded to have you, that he might sift you like wheat, but I have prayed for you that your faith may not fail; and when you have turned again, strengthen your brothers and sisters" (Luke 22:31–32). Peter denied knowing Jesus, but his faith in Jesus did not fail. Later he repented of his failure, and he used the story of his denial to strengthen his spiritual friends. The story of Peter's denial is in all four gospels (Matthew 26:69–75; Mark 14:66–72; Luke 22:54–62; John 18:25–27). In telling his story, Peter reminded future disciples of the message of grace: "If God can forgive me for what I did to Jesus, God will forgive your sins as well." He thus strengthened his brothers and sisters.

Jesus is our best friend. When we are assaulted by problems, we should turn to Jesus first. When our friends are in trouble, we need to take their burdens to Jesus.

Loving Our Friends

Some people view God as distant, unapproachable, demanding, and punitive. In Jesus, we see the face of a God who is present, approachable, accepting, and forgiving. God's love for us, revealed in Jesus, is unconditional (John 3:16). Jesus instructs us to marinate in his love: "As the Father has loved me, so have I loved you; abide in my love" (John 15:9). As the old song puts it, "Jesus loves me, this I know, for the Bible tells me so."

We are likewise to love our friends. Jesus puts this in the form of a command: "This is my commandment, that you love one another as I have loved you . . . You are my friends if you do what I command you . . . I am giving you this command so that you may love one another" (John 15:12, 14, 17). Paul says we are to love others with the love, which we have received from Jesus (Ephesians 4:32).

Love is a verb; it is something we do. We express our love for our friends in two ways:

1. Words. We tell our friends verbally how dear and precious they are to us. Why are we embarrassed to tell our friends that we care about them? Why is it so hard to say, "I love you"? Each of us has a deep need for verbal reassurance. It is hard for someone to overdo their expression of affection for us if it is genuine.

2. Deeds. Love is expressed in action. How do we know that Jesus Christ loves us? Because he laid down his life for us (John 15:13). Love is something we do. It is not an attitude or a feeling. It is an action with concrete manifestations. Paul tells us specifically what it means to be a loving person: "Love is patient; love is kind; love is not envious, or boastful, or arrogant, or rude. It does not insist on its own way; it is not irritable or resentful; it does not rejoice in wrongdoing, but rejoices in the truth. It bears all things, endures all things. Love never ends" (1 Corinthians 13:1–8).

I believe we treat other people the way we think God feels about us. Once you grasp this principle, you will begin to understand why there is so much religious hatred. Religious people can be the meanest people. Just because people sing about God's grace and talk about God's mercy doesn't mean they have internalized it. People who have not acknowledged love from God are unable to love others.

What is wrong with people who . . .

- Cannot love? They have not assimilated God's love.
- Cannot forgive? They have not received God's forgiveness.
- Cannot be generous? They believe they are on their own in a world of scarcity.

When we do not acknowledge God's love, forgiveness, and generosity, we can become hateful, unforgiving, and greedy people.

Now believe the good news: God loves you! God knows everything there is to know about you and loves you anyway. God loves you unconditionally, without reservation or condition.

Open your heart and allow God's love to be poured into your heart through the Holy Spirit (Romans 5:5). Let the love of God touch the core of your being. Abide in his love. Marinate in it. How can we receive the flow of God's Spirit? The holy wind of God comes the same way wind currents flow: from high pressure to low pressure. If you want the wind of God to fill you (John 3:8), you must get in a posture of low resistance. You must submit your will to the God who cares for you.

When you experience God's love, you will become a means by which God loves others.

Sacrificing for Our Friends

Jesus said, "No one has greater love than this, to lay down one's life for one's friend" (John 15:13). When Jesus spoke these words, he was about to be arrested and crucified. The cross is the greatest act of friendship in human history.

I love to read the stories of the brave American soldiers who have won the Congressional Medal of Honor. But Jesus' sacrifice was greater than the combined sacrifice of all those Medal of Honor winners. Those heroes put their lives in harm's way to save a few of their comrades, so that their comrades might have a chance to live another thirty, forty, or fifty years. Jesus died for all humanity so that we might live eternally (Romans 5:6–11).

Jesus gives us a wonderful example of friendship. Our friendship should extend to surrendering our lives on behalf of a friend (John 15:13). We will not get a Medal of Honor for it, but we will receive the approval of our heavenly Redeemer.

Friendship always has a degree of sacrifice related to it. When someone is our friend, we are willing to respond to his call in the middle of the night (Luke 11:5–8) and place his interests above our own (Philippians 2:4). When someone is our friend, we never use him to achieve some ulterior motive. Instead we keep his best interest at heart. This does not mean friendship is not fun. Friendship is a source of complete joy, according to Jesus (John 15:11).

We tend to think that laying down our lives means giving up our biological lives. But that would mean we could only give our lives once. There is more than one way to give up one's life, and we can do it many times over our lifetime. The simple act of listening, giving a friend our focused attention, is an example of laying down our life for a friend.

Another example of a sacrificial friendship is showing up when our friends are going through difficult times. We find out who our friends are when things are tough. Sometimes it is a crushing disappointment to discover that our friend is self-absorbed rather than self-sacrificial. On the other hand, there is nothing more strengthening than to have a friend show up in an hour of need.

Many years ago, when I was nearly killed in a serious accident, two friends interrupted their vacation and drove hundreds of miles to be with Susan at the hospital. They laid down their vacation for a friend. The Bible says it best: "A friend loves at all times, and (spiritual) kinfolks are born to share adversity" (Proverbs 17:17).

One of the greatest stories of sacrificial friendship loyalty took place in the final installment of the television epic

Lonesome Dove.[4] It is a story about two hard-bitten Texas Rangers who lived in the early nineteenth century, Captain Gus McCrae and Captain Woodrow Call. Together they had fought the Comanche Indians, arrested desperadoes, and helped to tame the Texas frontier. Gus accompanied Woodrow on a cattle drive from Southwest Texas to Montana to establish a cattle ranch. They traveled for months, contending with inclement weather and hostile Native Americans. Just as they were about to reach their destination, Gus was shot in both legs with arrows. Gangrene set in, and one of Gus' legs had to be removed. But Gus refused to have his other leg cut off, even though it would have saved his life. Woodrow arrived just before his friend died. Gus made him promise to take his body 3,000 miles back to Southwest Texas and bury him by a stream where he had once picnicked with the love of his life. It was an impractical request. But when spring came, Woodrow Call set out on the long journey. During the trip, Woodrow almost lost Gus's body in a savage river. When mocking people asked Woodrow to explain why he was doing such a ridiculous thing, he made this simple reply: "I told him I would."

We are all going to need a friend like Woodrow someday. Bad things will happen: illness, accidents, death, family problems, financial reversals. We will need someone to stand by us and be sacrificially loyal to us, no matter what it costs.

Sharing Secrets with Our Friends

Jesus said to his apostles, "I do not call you servants, because the servant does not know what his master is doing; but I have called you friends, because I have made known to you everything that I have heard from my Father" (John 15:15). Jesus was saying, "You are my friends because I have taken you into my confidence. I have given you access to my deepest secrets."

How do we know about Jesus' struggle with temptation in the wilderness of Judea (Matthew 4:1–11)? This event took place prior to the beginning of his ministry, before the call of any disciples. We know about it because Jesus must have disclosed it to his apostles, who recorded it.

In the same way, we risk sharing our secrets with friends. We tell friends our stories—the good ones and the bad ones. These friends treat our stories as precious gifts. Jesus said we are not to "throw pearls to swine" (Matthew 7:6). We do not share our secrets indiscriminately but carefully. Secrets are disclosed only to trusted friends.

Some of us would rather be admired for the self we appear to be than risk being loved for the self we really are. We will do almost anything to hold on to a public persona. Impression-management traps us in shallow relationships, and it guarantees that we will remain alone. It forces us to keep wearing masks, to appear to be people we are not. And chronic inauthenticity makes it impossible to have what we need most: intimate friendships.

Someone has said that we never know who we are until we tell someone else who we think we are, and they interpret back to us who we really are. We need friends who will listen patiently as we disclose the painful facts about ourselves and then give us an objective perspective.

Swiss psychiatrist Paul Tournier wrote a book titled *Secrets*. He said it was normal and developmentally appropriate for adolescents to keep secrets from their parents.[5] If they never keep secrets, then intimacy never means anything to them, because intimacy involves disclosing secrets. Tournier went on to say that as young people mature, it is normal for them to find trustworthy people and begin to share their secrets.[6] Unfortunately, many adults never cross this maturity threshold.

One of the things psychotherapists marvel at is that patients will visit with them for years, paying large fees to do so, yet withhold the one vital piece of information the therapist needs in order to understand and help the patient. These therapeutic patients just cannot manage to disclose their biggest secrets.

James tells us to confess our faults to one another (James 5:16). Friendship allows us to dare to be truthful about our sinfulness. When we pretend to be sinless, we are liars; when we confess our sins, fellowship takes place (1 John 1:6–10). When we share our secrets, it encourages other people to come out of hiding and share their secrets as well.

What a relief it is to allow feelings long trapped in the basement of our souls to be released. Buried in our gut, these feelings get bigger and become more powerful. When secrets are allowed to touch the air, they lose their power over us. How healing it is to allow these feelings to come out unmeasured, without worrying about how they sound, knowing that the ones who hear them will love us still.

AA teaches people in recovery that secrets make us sick: "You are only as sick as your secrets." If no one knows our secrets, we are both sick and friendless. Conversely, when we share our secrets with trustworthy people, we receive both healing and community. We are no longer trapped in sickness.

Of course, sharing secrets is dangerous if the person to whom we are risking transparency is not capable of keeping confidences. The Bible warns against telling secrets to a gossip (Proverbs 20:19). For example, Samson made a poor choice in sharing the secret of his strength with Delilah, who was interested only in his defeat and humiliation (Judges 16:1–22). We must be wise and discerning before entrusting our souls to other persons.

Placing Financial Resources
at the Disposal of Our Friends

Jesus said, "I have appointed you to go and bear fruit, fruit that will last, so that the Father will give you whatever you ask in my name" (John 15:16). Jesus gave his apostles power of attorney to ask God for whatever they needed. Why did he give them this privilege? Because they were his closest friends, and friends make their resources available to one another.

Jesus had no possessions except the clothes on his back (Mark 15:24). Generous people allowed him to borrow things—a colt (Mark 11:2–7); a large, furnished upstairs room (Mark 14:12–16); a prayer garden (Mark 24:32); and an unused tomb hewn out of stone (Mark 15:42–46).

Friends are willing to share their resources with one another—time, energy, influence, wisdom, expertise, wealth. Jesus said the same thing to his friends. He essentially told them, "All that is mine is yours. You mean more to me than anything I possess."

A wise and wealthy man once made me a promise: "If you ever need anything, I will give it to you—provided I can give it to you and it will be good for you for me to give it." One day it occurred to me that I can make the same promise to my friends. I can offer to do anything for them—provided it is something I can do and it would be good for them for me to do it. Jesus offers us this caliber of friendship, and it is this kind of friendship we can offer to others.

I urge you to allow Jesus to be your friend. Jesus will be a perfect gentleman. He will not force himself on you. He will not inject his love into your soul as a doctor injects medicine. You have to be willing to say yes to Jesus' offer of friendship. Jesus does not want to be your friend because he needs something from you; he wants to be your friend because he loves you.

Jesus will be a loyal friend. He will understand your humanity (Hebrews 2:18). He will give you care. He will never abuse you or abandon you. And his indwelling presence will help you to be the person you want to be (John 14:17). In addition, the Holy Spirit will guide you in your search for Jesus-type friends.

There is going to come a time when your greatest treasure will not be your bank account or the toys you have collected. Your most important asset will be your friends. I hope you will be wise enough to make the kind of friendship investments that will sustain you when that day comes. And like job hunting, the best time to look for a friend is before you need one.

A FINAL REMINDER

In chapter 1, I recounted a dream I came to see as a revelation from God. Through the dream, God seemed to be saying to me, "Jim, you have mistakenly defined yourself as a loner. That is a distorted image of your true identity. From now on, define yourself as a relational person—a person with intimate relationships. Now come out of hiding, open up to other people, and enjoy genuine friends. You have nothing to fear. You will never walk alone again." I have been seeking to be obedient to this heavenly vision ever since (Acts 26:19).

The message contained in my dream is as much for the loners reading this book as it is for me. Do not wait for a dream. Take these printed words as God's message to you.

You are not a loner anymore! From now on, you have permission to walk away from this distorted self-image and live a life of interconnected covenant friendships.

Discussion Questions and Activities

Chapter 1: The Loner's Plight
Scripture Lesson—Genesis 1; 2 Corinthians 3:12–18

Applying the Word
Read Genesis 1 and 2 Corinthians 3:12–18 as a guide to understanding where you are in the spiritual transformation process.

For Personal Reflection
1. Draw a timeline of your life, noting milestone events in your spiritual pilgrimage.
2. When did you first realize you were alone in the world? Describe your age and the circumstance.
3. What personal or secondhand experiences have you had with addictive disorders?
4. Study the twelve steps listed in chapter 1. Which of these steps do you need to work? What is holding you back from taking these steps in your life?
5. Reflect on the statement, "We are not able to think ourselves into new ways of behaving; we have to behave ourselves into a new way of thinking." Name one action you will take

this week that will lead you to a behavior change that is consistent with your thinking.

For Group Discussion
1. Describe a positive and a negative experience from your childhood that still affects you.
2. Describe the masks you wore as a child or young adult as a defense mechanism in order to please the important people in your life or to fit in with a peer group.
3. Are you a loner? If so, why? If not, why not?
4. What small-group experiences have you had that could be described as spiritual and intimate? If you are studying this book with a group, decide together how you will share your thoughts and experiences in a trusting, open, respectful way.

Just for Fun with Your Group
Make masks out of poster boards. Decorate the masks in ways that visually represent who you often pretend to be.

Chapter 2: Loneliness vs. All Rightness
Scripture Lesson—Ecclesiastes 4:7–12; 1 John 1:5–10

Applying the Word
Ecclesiastes 4:9–12 points out our need for human relationships. First John 1:5–10 describes the divine friendship we can have with God. Read these passages and reflect on your current relationships. With whom are you bound in a three-fold cord? Who lifts you up when you fall, and who are you willing to lift up? God desires a transparent relationship with you. Are you in the habit of confessing your sin to your trustworthy Creator, who loves you and forgives you?

For Personal Reflection

1. Have you ever experienced developmental loneliness? How? If not, have you known someone who has? What was their experience?
2. What forms of environmental loneliness have you experienced; e.g., urbanization, mobilization, computerization, singularization, individualization? What was your experience?
3. Have you ever used an addictive agent to numb the pain of existential loneliness? When? What were the circumstances?

For Group Discussion

1. Reflect together on the words of Thomas Wolfe: "The whole conviction of my life now rests upon the belief that loneliness, far from being a rare and curious phenomenon, particular to myself and a few other men, is the central and inevitable fact of human existence." In what sense do you believe he is right? How does seeing this perspective make you feel?
2. Give an example of a time when a friendship caused pain in your life.
3. What spiritual disciplines would you like to develop that would help you develop divine companionship? Covenant with your group to pursue prayer, journaling, Bible reading and/or study, devotional reading, fasting, financial generosity, attending worship, or serving others this week.
4. How could you alter your schedule to create time for solitude with God? How could things such as silence, stillness, simplicity, and Sabbath enhance your solitude with God?

Just for Fun with Your Group

Have someone read aloud Ecclesiastes 4:9–12. In groups of two, create a role-play scenario for each of the four examples in this passage.

Chapter 3: The Beauty of Covenant Friendship
Scripture Lesson—1 Samuel 18:1–4; 23:15–18

Applying the Word
Read 1 Samuel 13–31 in a contemporary translation of the Bible. Read quickly, absorbing this portion of Israel's history. Look for what you learn about the character and nature of God. What traits do you see in David and in Jonathan? How would you describe their relationships with God, with one another, and with others? What can you apply to your own relationship with God and with others from this portion of Scripture?

For Personal Reflection
1. Do you recognize the need for a covenant friendship? Why or why not?
2. If you are married, are you currently in a covenant friendship with anyone other than your spouse? If so, who?
3. What needs do you have that might be met through a covenant friendship?
4. What specific things frighten you most about entering a covenant friendship?

For Group Discussion
1. If you were looking for a covenant friend, which characteristics would you seek?
2. When choosing a friend, especially a covenant friend, several factors affect our decisions. Discuss with your group how the following criteria might influence your relationship:
a. Gender
b. Socio/economic/cultural background
c. Personal chemistry
3. In what ways could entering a covenant friendship be sacrificial for you? What would friendship with you call on someone else to sacrifice?

Just for Fun with Your Group
As a group, write the outline of a friendship covenant ritual. Discuss what specific words and symbolic deeds should be part of it. Respect all contributions to the process. Think about how you might tweak the ritual for your personal preferences, just as many couples write their own marriage vows.

Chapter 4: Hurts and Healings
Scripture Lesson—Genesis 2:18; 3:1–13, 20–21

Applying the Word
Read the account of God's friendship with Adam and Eve in Genesis 2:18; 3:1–13, 20–21. Go back over the ways God related to Adam and Eve as the friend taking the initiative, asking questions, telling the truth, hanging in there, and respecting boundaries. With which of these characteristics do you have the most trouble, either in your relationship with God or in your human relationships?

For Personal Reflection
1. Give an example of a time when fear, shame, blaming, pretending, or denial prevented you from having a healthy friendship.
2. Make a list of the five most negative and hurtful things that have ever been said to you—who said them, what they said, and when they were said. Then make a list of the five most positive and affirming things that have ever been said to you— who said them, what they said, and when they were said. Reflect on how these 10 people have influenced your life.

For Group Discussion
1. Find someone you do not know well and share the timeline you created in Week One with them.

2. Next, form groups of six to eight persons. Have each person introduce their partner to the group by means of the timeline. Take turns until everyone is introduced.
3. If we, like Lazarus, need people to unwrap us and set us free, who are the people who are unwrapping you? How are they unwrapping you?
4. Part of this chapter is devoted to boundaries. Discuss something negative that has happened to you because an appropriate boundary was not drawn. What boundaries do you need? Covenant with your group to begin setting a healthy boundary in one relationship this week.

Just for Fun with Your Group

Draw the outline of a person on a piece of poster board. Go around the group developing the composite of an ideal friend. Each person should add a characteristic and tell why they think it is important. Prioritize the qualities as a group. Discuss whether or not you are willing to be this kind of friend to someone. Remember that the list you just prioritized is not a job description for someone else.

Chapter 5: How to Choose Friends Wisely
Scripture Lesson— Job 2:1–22; Mark 2:1–12

Applying the Word

Read Mark 2:1–12. Imagine you are one of the characters in the story. What is your greatest need at this time in your life? Do you need friends to bring you to Jesus? Do you need to bring a friend to the Healer? Do you need forgiveness? Do you have a physical need? Do you relate more to the bystanders in this story? Is there some part of you that is doubtful of Jesus' ability to heal and forgive? Let this story soak into your soul.

thus and so to me, and more as well, even if death parts me from you" (Ruth 1:16-17). What part of a covenant like this would you be willing to make? What part makes you uncomfortable? Can you imagine yourself making a one-way covenant with someone? Why or why not?

3. The chapter points out six relational words that help friendships flourish. Which one of these will you commit to doing this week? Share with the group how you will pursue allegiance, acceptance, availability, affirmation, attention, or accountability in one of your covenant relationships.

4. Find a group of people with whom you can answer Chuck Swindoll's accountability questions. What accountability questions could be added? What about adding this question: "What is it that you most do not want to tell me?"

Just for Fun with Your Group

Naomi tried to give herself the name Mara when she was at her lowest point. Jesus gave new names of encouragement to Peter and Paul. Think for a minute what new name would you like for Jesus to give you. As a group, read Revelation 2:17 together and give one another new names that reflect the spiritual gifts you see in one another.

Chapter 7: Friendship Fatality
Scripture Lesson—Acts 14:8–18; Galatians 6:1–5

Applying the Word

Pray and ask God to guide you by the Holy Spirit as you read Galatians 6:1–5. What do you discern is your current burden in life? What is your load or ordinary responsibility? How is God calling you to respond to this text in your own life and in your relationships with others?

For Personal Reflection
1. Write down your three most pressing life situations. Label them as burdens or loads. Do you need to ask for help? Do you need to assume more responsibility for this situation?
2. Define codependency in your own words.
3. Evaluate your reaction to this motto: "If I don't do it, it won't get done."
4. Reflect on the priority you place on your own needs and the needs of your family, friends, and coworkers.

For Group Discussion
1. Give an example of a time you were under a crushing load and you needed a friend to help you lift your burden.
2. Someone has said the three rules of codependency are don't ask, don't tell, and don't feel. Discuss why these three rules would be toxic.
3. Discuss a time when you did something to help someone out and it destroyed the relationship. If it has not happened to you, discuss someone you know to whom this has happened.

Just for Fun with Your Group
In groups of three, create three-minute impromptu skits that dramatize situations in which a person feels responsible for carrying loads that are not his or hers to carry. Discuss the skits in the large group.

Close your time together by reading the "Serenity Prayer." Ask each person to reflect on which petition is the hardest to accept.

"God, grant me the serenity to accept the things I cannot change, The courage to change the things I can, And the wisdom to know the difference."

Consider attending a CODA or an AL-ANON meeting. This could be a group field trip.

Chapter 8: A Fond Farewell?
Scripture Lesson—Acts 15:36–41; 2 Timothy 4:6–13

Applying the Word
Read Acts 15:36–41 and 2 Timothy 4:6–13. How does the story of Barnabas and Paul's disagreement over ministry and their eventual split make you feel? Why do you think this happened? What does this story tell us about people and relationships?

For Personal Reflection
1. Reflect on one or two persons you knew only briefly who had a profound effect on your life. Offer a prayer of thanksgiving for that meaningful relationship.
2. If you have experienced the breakup of a friendship, reflect on the cause of the split. Which category mentioned in the chapter was the source? What did you learn from that time in your life?
3. The chapter mentions that we all have blind spots when it comes to relationships. Do you struggle with any of the ones mentioned? Can you name any others?

For Group Discussion
1. How do the covenantal images of sacrament, trinity, marriage, and adoption affect your thinking about terminating relationships?
2. Discuss how the following life changes can destroy friendships: marriage, divorce, death, drifting, blind spots.
3. Discuss the difference between forgiveness and reconciliation and how confusion between the two leads people to have false guilt.
4. Discuss how the problem with reconciliation is often our lack of desire for it. Give examples from your life when this has been real for you.

Just for Fun with Your Group

As a group, simulate calling someone to a peace conference. Conclude the session with prayer for relationships that are in jeopardy. If necessary and appropriate, use the Joyce Rupp prayer at the end of the chapter. Commit to continue in prayer for one another.

Chapter 9: You've Got a Friend
Scripture Lesson—Mark 3:13–19; John 15:9–17

Applying the Word

Chapter 9 includes the author's paraphrase of John 15:4–5. Read John 15:9–17 and rewrite verses 4–5 in your own words. From that passage, make a list of some practical things you could do to become more intentionally connected to Jesus. Ask God for a word or a phrase from the passage that you can meditate on during the week ahead.

For Personal Reflection

1. Take a large sheet of paper and draw four concentric circles on it, one representing each of the four types of relationships in Jesus' life. Place the names of the friends that fit in each category on the sheet.

    a. Does the time you spend with these people reflect the value you place on the relationship? If not, what should you do about it?

    b. Which relationship on the circle would you like to see grow into greater intimacy? What should you do about it?

    c. Is there someone in the circle with whom you share your secrets? If your answer is no, why not? Do you have secrets you have never shared with anyone? What prevents you from telling a friend your secrets? What is your greatest fear about telling the secrets? If you were to tell a friend, which friend should it be? What kind of relief would it give you to share the secrets with someone trustworthy?

2. Spend a few minutes writing a paraphrase of 1 Corinthians 13:1–8. With which of these characteristics do you have the most problems?

For Group Discussion

1. What does the concept of being "in Christ" mean to you?
2. In what way has Jesus been a friend to you?
3. Describe a time when someone "was Jesus to you."
4. Describe a time when you made a sacrifice for a friend—either in time, prayer, financially, or an act of service.

Just for Fun with Your Group

Form pairs to read aloud 1 Corinthians 13:1–8 together. Have one person read the passage, changing the word *love* to the other person's name. Switch roles and read the passage again. Discuss with your partner how you felt as your name was associated with each description for love.

NOTES

Introduction
1. Aelred of Rievaulx, Spiritual Friendship (Kalamazoo, MI: Cistercian Press, 1977), 58–61.
2. Used with permission from the author.

Chapter 1: The Loner's Plight
1. Alcoholics Anonymous: The Story of How Many Men and Women Have Recovered from Alcoholism (New York: Alcoholics Anonymous World Service, 1976), 509.
2. Ibid., 59–60.

Chapter 2: Loneliness vs. All Rightness
1. Thomas Wolfe, The Hills Beyond (New York: Harper and Brothers, 1941), 186.
2. Edgar N. Jackson, Understanding Loneliness (Philadelphia: Fortress Press, 1980), 19–26.
3. Ibid., 46.
4. Jacques Ellul, The Meaning of the City (Grand Rapids: Eerdmans, 1970), 15–20.

5. Ronald Rolheiser, The Restless Heart: Finding Our Spiritual Home in Times of Loneliness (New York: Doubleday, 2004), 8.
6. Ronald Rolheiser, Everything Belongs: The Gift of Contemplative Prayer (New York: Crossroads, 2003), 79.
7. Paul Wadell, Becoming Friends: Worship, Justice, and the Practice of Christian Friendship (Grand Rapids: Brazos Press, 2002), 44.
8. C. S. Lewis, The Four Loves (New York: Harcourt Brace Jovanovich, 1960), 2.
9. Ronald Rolheiser, The Restless Heart: Finding Our Spiritual Home in Times of Loneliness, 3.
10. Nicholas A. Christakis and James H. Fowler, Connected: How Your Friends' Friends' Friends Affect Everything You Do (New York: Little Brown and Company, 2009), 236.
11. Ibid., 57.
12. T. S. Eliot, Selected Poems (New York: Harcourt, Brace and World, 1964), 114.
13. Blaise Pascal, Pensees (New York: E. P. Dutton and Co., 1958), 155.
14. Ronald Rolheiser, Ibid., 111.
15. Nicholas A. Christakis and James H. Fowler, Connected, 243.

Chapter 3: The Beauty of Covenant Friendship

1. Aristotle, Nicomachean Ethic, W. D. Ross, trans. (MobileReference, 2010), book 8, section 3; 1982.
2. Ronald Rolheiser, Forgotten Among the Lilies: Learning to Love Beyond Our Fears (New York: Doubleday, 2004), 36.
3. Theodore F. Adams, Making Your Marriage Succeed (New York: Harper and Brothers, 1953), 16.
4. Liz Carmichael, Friendship: Interpreting Christian Love (New York: T & T Clark, 2004), 48.

5. Bryan Patrick McGuire, Friendship and Community: the Monastic Experience, 350–1250 (Kalamazoo, MI: Cistercian Press, 1988), 383, 386.
6. Joseph Epstein, Friendship: An Exposé (New York: Houghton Mifflin, 2006), 8.
7. John Boswell, Same-Sex Unions in Premodern Europe (New York: Vintage, 1995), 262.
8. Ibid., 215.
9. Ibid., 185, 191, 193–94, 206–207, 209–10, 215–17.
10. Robert Bain, Friends and Lovers (New York: Basic Books, 1976), 91.
11. John Boswell, Same-Sex Unions in Premodern Europe, 291–306, 311–23, 327–41.
12. Robert Bain, Friends and Lovers, 91.
13. John Boswell, Same-Sex Unions in Premodern Europe, 178.
14. Robert Bain, Friends and Lovers, 91.

Chapter 4: Hurts and Healings

1. Paul Wadell, Becoming Friends: Worship, Justice, and the Practice of Christian Friendship (Grand Rapids: Brazos Press, 2002), 41.
2. William Shakespeare, Hamlet (Champaign, Il.: Project Gutenberg, 1999), Act III, p. 170.
3. D. J. Enright and David Rawlinson, The Oxford Book of Friendship (New York: Oxford University Press, 1991), 29.
4. Robert Frost, Complete Poems of Robert Frost (New York: St. Martin's Paperbacks, 1971), 97.
5. Kahlil Gibran, The Prophet (New York: Alfred A. Knopf, 1951), 15.
6. Ralph Earle and Susan Metsner, Come Here, Go Away (New York: Simon and Schuster, 1991), 10.

Chapter 5: How to Choose Friends Wisely

1. Aelred of Rievaulx, Spiritual Friendship (Kalamazoo, MI: Cistercian Press, 1977), 78.
2. James I. Robertson Jr., ed., Stonewall Jackson's Book of Maxims (Nashville: Cumberland House, 2002), 14.
3. Keith R. Anderson, Friendships That Run Deep (Downers Grove, IL: InterVarsity, 1997), 58.
4. Paul D. O'Callaghan, The Feast of Friendship (Wichita, KS: Eighth Day Press, 2002), 19.
5. Donald X. Burt, Friendship and Society: An Introduction to Augustine's Practical Philosophy (Grand Rapids: Eerdmans, 1999), 62.
6. Joseph Epstein, Friendship: An Exposé (New York: Houghton Mifflin, 2006), 24.
7. Samuel Francis Woodard, The Beauties of Friendship (Wichita, KS: Goldsmith Book and Stationery, 1906), 36.
8. Hugh Prather, Notes to Myself (Moab, UT: Real People Press, 1970), 103.
9. D. J. Enright and David Rawlinson, The Oxford Book of Friendship (New York, Oxford University Press, 1991), 349.
10. "Net Fax," Carol Childress, ed. Tyler, TX. Leadership Network, No. 20, "Retooling the Church"; May 29, 1995.
11. Sault K. Padover, Jefferson (New York: Harcourt Brace Jovanovich, 1970), 164.

Chapter 6: Friendship . . . for the Moment or Forever?

1. Joseph Epstein, Friendship: An Exposé (New York: Houghton Mifflin, 2006), 96.
2. Aristotle, Nicomachean Ethic, W. D. Ross, trans. (MobileReference, 2010), book 8, section 12; 210.
3. D. J. Enright and David Rawlinson, The Oxford Book of Friendship (New York, Oxford University Press, 1991), 205.
4. Nicholas A. Christakis and James H. Fowler, Connected:

How Your Friends' Friends' Friends Affect Everything You Do (New York: Little Brown and Company, 2009), 10.

5. Guy Greenfield, We Need Each Other: Reaching a Deeper Level in Our Interpersonal Relationships (Grand Rapids: Baker, 1984), 78.

6. George Barna, Revolution (Carol Stream, IL: Tyndale, 2005), 34.

7. Charles R. Swindoll, Rise and Shine (Portland, OR: Multnomah, 1989), 211.

Chapter 7: Friendship Fatality

1. Melody Beattie, Codependent No More: How to Stop Controlling Others and Start Caring for Yourself (Center City, MN: Hazelden Foundation, 1987), 32.

2. Aelred of Rievaulx., Spiritual Friendship (Kalamazoo, MI: Cistercian Press, 1977), 87.

3. Carmen Renee Barry, When Helping You Is Hurting Me! Escaping the Messiah Trap (San Francisco: Harper and Row, 1988), 6.

4. Ibid., 57.

Chapter 8: A Fond Farewell?

1. Ann Hibhard, Treasured Friends: Finding and Keeping True Friends (Grand Rapids: Baker, 1997), 158.

2. Blaise Pascal, Pensees (New York: E. P. Dutton and Co., 1958), 137–38.

3. Aristotle, Nicomachean Ethic, W. D. Ross, trans. (MobileReference, 2010), book 8, section 5; 197.

4. Carmen L. Caltagirone, Friendship as Sacrament (New York: Alba House, 1988), 37.

5. Ibid., 7.

6. Laura Davis, I Thought We'd Never Speak Again (New York: Harper Collins, 2002), 3.

7. Aelred of Rievaulx, Spiritual Friendship (Kalamazoo, MI: Cistercian Press, 1977), 93.

8. Ibid., 59.

9. Kenneth E. Bailey, Poet and Peasant and through Peasant Eyes (Grand Rapids: Eerdmans, 1983), 167–168.

10. Joyce Rupp, Praying Our Goodbyes: A Spiritual Companion through Life's Losses and Sorrows (Notre Dame, IN: Ave Marie Press, 2009), 130.

Chapter 9: You've Got a Friend

1. Joseph M. Scriven, "What a Friend We Have in Jesus," United Methodist Hymnal (Nashville: United Methodist Publishing House, 1989), No. 526.

2. Aristotle, Nicomachean Ethic, W. D. Ross, trans. (MobileReference, 2010), book 8, section 3; 1982.

3. Wolfgang Meider, ed., Encyclopedia of World Proverbs (Englewood Cliffs, N.J.: Prentice Hall, 1986), 180.

4. Carmen L. Caltagirone, Friendship as Sacrament (New York: Albu House, 1988), 93.

5. Lonesome Dove; based on novel by Larry McMurtry; teleplay by Bill Witliff; Cabin Fever Entertainment, 1991.

6. Paul Tournier, Secrets (Richmond, VA: John Knox Press, 1963), 6–16.

7. Ibid., 28-39.

ABOUT THE AUTHOR

Dr. James (Jim) F. Jackson was a pastor for many years in Georgia and Texas. He served as Senior Pastor of Chapelwood United Methodist Church in Houston, Texas, from 1994 to 2014. Dr. Jackson now devotes his full time to writing, teaching, and life coaching in Houston, where he lives with his watercolorist wife, Susan. His popular blog, Jim's Daily Awakenings (www.jimsdailyawakenings.com), is widely read by thousands across the United States and around the world. He can be reached at jim@equip3.com.

OTHER BOOKS BY DR. JAMES F. (JIM) JACKSON

Good News by a Man Named Mark
Lessons From Life
More Lessons From Life